Will of the People

A FREEDOM HOUSE BOOK

Recent Titles in Studies in Freedom

Strategies for the 1980s: Lessons of Cuba, Vietnam, and Afghanistan
Philip van Slyck

Escape to Freedom: The Story of the International Rescue Committee
Aaron Levenstein

Forty Years: A Third World Soldier at the UN
Carlos P. Romulo with Beth Day Romulo

Will of the People

Original Democracy in Non-Western Societies

Raul S. Manglapus

STUDIES IN FREEDOM, NUMBER 4

Greenwood Press
New York • Westport, Connecticut • London

Library of Congress Cataloging-in-Publication Data

Manglapus, Raúl S.
   Will of the people.

   (Studies in freedom, ISSN 0732-6610 ; no. 4)
   Includes index.
   1. Democracy—Case studies. I. Title.
II. Series.
JC421.M34   1987   321.8'092'6   86-29594
ISBN 0-313-25837-6 (lib. bdg. : alk. paper)

Copyright © 1987 by Freedom House

All rights reserved. No portion of this book may be
reproduced, by any process or technique, without the
express written consent of the publisher.

Library of Congress Catalog Card Number: 86-29594
ISBN: 0-313-25837-6
ISSN: 0732-6610

First published in 1987

Greenwood Press, Inc.
88 Post Road West, Westport, Connecticut 06881

Printed in the United States of America

The paper used in this book complies with the
Permanent Paper Standard issued by the National
Information Standards Organization (Z39.48-1984).

10 9 8 7 6 5 4 3 2 1

Every reasonable effort has been made to trace the owners of copyright
materials in this book, but in some instances this has proven impossible.
The publishers will be glad to receive information leading to more complete
acknowledgments in subsequent printings of the book and in the meantime
extend their apologies for any omissions.

To that "inexperienced housewife," Corazon C. Aquino, who has shown the world that democracy is a native human right to be exercised, not a lesson that needs to be learned.

Contents

Foreword		ix
Preface		xiii
Acknowledgments		xxiii
Introduction		xxv
1	Democracy and Despotism: Chicken and Egg?	1
2	Marx and Toynbee *vs.* the "Cake of Custom"	11
3	Mesopotamia: Earliest Formal Democracy?	19
4	India: The Spirit of Licchavis	27
5	The Stubborn Village	35
6	The *Panchayat*: Gandhi *vs.* Britain	41
7	*Varna* and *Pygmalion*	47
8	Confucius Said...?	53
9	The Hills Are Alive	61
10	The *Adat*—Durable Cake	67
11	Stone Age Legislatures	77
12	The Consensual Islands	81

13	Iroquois—the First American Republic	89
14	The Tribes: Proving Jefferson Right	101
15	Aztecs: Mexican Schizophrenia	109
16	Incan Empire: The Democratic Fringe	119
17	Bantu Assembly: Original South African Democracy	125
18	One-Party System: Un-African Activity	133
19	Semitic Pluralism	145
20	Korea and Japan—the "Improbable Democracies?"	155
Index		163

Foreword

Democratic roots, and the nurturing of freedom in traditional, developing societies is Raul Manglapus's theme.

In his active life—a mixture of idealism and pragmatic political service—he has experienced the broad possibilities of freedom and the utter cruelty and degradation of tyranny. Since World War II interrupted his studies, Manglapus has been near the center of the action in the Pacific basin. But his concern has always included, as well, the aspirations of those struggling for the freedom of other lands in Africa, Eastern Europe, Latin America, and the mainland of Asia. By the time this volume appears, the author may once again have been elected a Senator in the restored democracy of the Philippines.

We first met shortly after he went into self-imposed exile following the declaration of martial law in 1972. From that moment Manglapus sought ways to resist the Marcos regime, restore democratic institutions, and simultaneously assist Yugoslavs, Cubans, Koreans, Taiwanese, and others fighting similar tyrannies. He became president of a group of freedom-inspired activists who came from the broad center of the political spectrum. They called themselves The Democracy International. Freedom House was pleased to assist at its birth.

This book reflects a similar objective: to demonstrate that there are indigenous roots of democracy in many traditional, developing societies; and that intellectual and political leaders, no matter how diverse their national heritages, can find common cause as members of the freedom party.

Manglapus dedicated himself to such objectives early in life. When the war in the Pacific struck at his homeland he left law school and joined the American armed forces as a broadcaster. He was imprisoned by the Japanese in 1942, but escaped two years later. He joined the Hunters Guerrillas attached to the U.S. 11th Airborne Division, served as captain, and later a war correspondent at General MacArthur's headquarters. He covered the Japanese surrender aboard the USS *Missouri* in Tokyo Bay.

After the war, Manglapus pursued the possibilities of democratizing his homeland as well as the region. He became secretary-general in 1954 of the founding conference of the Southeast Asia Treaty Organization (SEATO), and the following year vice-chairman of the Philippine delegation to the Asian-African Conference at Bandung, Indonesia (the origin of the Nonaligned Movement).

In 1957, at the age of 38, Raul Manglapus became (if only briefly) the youngest Secretary of Foreign Affairs in Philippine history. He entered the Senate in 1961 with a record number of votes. He sponsored a land reform code, and was named Most Outstanding Senator in 1963 and 1964. Again leading the winning senatorial list in 1970, he was elected delegate to the Constitutional Convention, became leader of the Progressive Party, and later of the Christian Social Movement.

In his public life, Manglapus has strived to create and bolster democratic institutions. He has sought to blend the highest spirit of the traditional world with the tested political implements of developed, industrial lands. When Ferdinand Marcos made political freedom untenable in the Philippines, Manglapus took up residence in the United States and founded the Movement for a Free Philippines. He then became a visiting professor at Cornell University (1973–74), engaged in research at the Carnegie Endowment for International Peace (1974–75), taught at American University (1977–80), headed the Center for Development Policy in Washington (1982), and was a fellow at the Center for International Affairs at Harvard University (1985).

All of these interests were combined in the project Manglapus undertook for Freedom House in 1983: the study of non-Western democratic traditions. His travels took him to Asia, Africa, Latin America, and indigenous United States.

Freedom House was interested in this study because it complemented our own continuing analysis of the level of political rights and civil liberties in every country and related territory. This analysis, conducted by Raymond D. Gastil, is published annually as a part of the annual *Freedom in the World: Political Rights and Civil Liberties.**

We construct criteria for human freedom that can be applied universally, whether the country is a traditional, agrarian society or among the most modern industrial nations. We employ the tools of political science, tempered with judgments made by comparing similar societies.

Manglapus's study moves along a far lengthier time frame. He delves more deeply into the past to discover the roots of democratic stirrings. He employs his special idealism and commitment to show how it is possible to accommodate traditional culture to the needs of modern societies; by enhancing human freedom without the loss of particular mores—economic, social or political—that distinguish one people from another.

Leonard R. Sussman
Executive Director, Freedom House

---

*Raymond D. Gastil, editor and principal author. Published by Greenwood Press; latest edition : 1986–1987. See also the bimonthly *Freedom at Issue*, January-February numbers, 1973 through 1987.

Preface

On February 25, 1986, borne on the shoulders of what is now proudly proclaimed as "people power," the Philippines were put back on the road to democracy.

It was not the first time in the last decade or so that a dictatorship had been forced out of government by a massed, marching population. In 1973, almost half a million Thai marched down the streets of Bangkok demanding an end to the then-ruling triumvirate military dictatorship. The army killed sixty-five of them, then stopped firing and told the dictators to go away. The king stepped in, appointed a nonpolitical university professor provisional prime minister to supervise elections, and in one year Thailand was a working democracy. Three years later, the fragile springtime of freedom was to give way to one more military dictatorship.

Since then, however, fourteen countries have moved from right-wing dictatorships to more promisingly stable constitutional democracies, in chronological order: Greece, Portugal, Spain, India, the Dominican Republic, Ecuador, Peru, Bolivia, Honduras, Argentina, Uruguay, Brazil, Guatemala, and the Philippines.

On a fellowship at the Center for International Affairs at Harvard University in 1985, I had occasion to study all these transitions, with the exception of that of Guatemala, which was accomplished after the end of my research. In each case, it was popular protest and pressure in varying forms and intensities that initiated the process of dismantling repressive rule and completing a successful transition to democracy.

Sometimes, the final collapse of the dictatorship was precipitated by military adventurism abroad—the Greeks in Cyprus, the Portuguese in Angola and Mozambique, the Argentinians in the Malvinas. In any case, peaceful or relatively bloodless transition became irreversible only when the Armed Forces decided to "join" the people and withdraw support of the dictatorship.

The cooperation and sometimes-shared leadership of other national institutions also was important and even essential for success. For example, all but three of the fourteen transitions took place in predominantly Roman Catholic countries, and there the Church, once popularly regarded as conservative, invariably turned into a crucial propellant for democratic change.

As early as March, 1984, I had predicted before the Los Angeles World Affairs Council a scenario for a Philippine democratic transition:

1. the awakened democratic movement marches in a massive appeal to the Armed Forces;
2. democratic leaders stand up to offer themselves formally as an alternative to the dictatorship;
3. the Armed Forces join the leaders and the people and support a transition government composed of representatives of all the democratic sectors, including the Muslims;
4. the Church morally supports the transition government;
5. the transition government holds a referendum for the people to express their choice of constitution;
6. the transition government holds elections under the chosen constitution;
7. the elected officials take office.

The Philippine democratic movement really had never been dormant through the years of the dictatorship, which had begun in September, 1972. However, it had been forced underground and into exile. The international press kept the world informed of the thousands in detention camps and thousands more "salvaged" (the Philippine colloquial euphemism for being made to disappear), live and dead witnesses to a vibrant and stubborn democratic drive among the Filipino people. Abroad, especially in the United States, exile democratic organizations, the first one being the Movement for a Free Philippines, reenacted the historic role of the Philippine propaganda movement in Spain one hundred years ago.

The intensity of Philippine "people power," however, began to outgrow and outpace that of its counterparts in other countries when the Marcos government committed a mistake which other dictatorships had theretofore carefully avoided. The worst that dictatorships had been doing to returning exile leaders was to detain them. However, on August 21, 1983, Benigno Aquino, Jr., returning from exile in the United States, was summarily executed as he descended from his plane at the Manila International Airport.

Millions instantly poured out into the streets in protest against the assassination. Objective observers estimated that when Aquino's body was brought from the capital city of Manila to his hometown one hundred miles north, about 7 million people lined the highways (the Philippines' 600 inhabited islands are populated by 54 million people). The Philippine democratic movement had surfaced at last with a momentum that Marcos would never be able to control.

In a theatrical demonstration of accommodation to domestic and international pressure, Marcos appointed a civilian "nonpartisan" commission to investigate the Aquino assassination. The ploy boomeranged when the commission, with its handpicked chairperson dissenting, found twenty-six members of the Armed Forces, including the chief of staff, Gen. Fabian Ver, indictable for the offense.

The trial was then assigned to the *tanodbayan*, a sort of ombudsman group whose original official task was to process people's complaints and whose very specially chosen members promptly exonerated Ver. By this time, an overconfident Marcos had called for a "snap" presidential election, thinking that he could count on a weak and divided opposition and a demoralized electorate that could be expected passively to accept manufactured results in his favor as in the past during his thirteen-year dictatorship. It was to be for him a fatal miscalculation; for the people, it was to be a long-awaited moment of challenge and opportunity.

In my predicted scenario, I had visualized democratic elections coming not at the beginning but at the end of the transition process, after the massed population, with the ultimate support of the Armed Forces and the Church, had ousted the dictatorship. I had predicted correctly that elections in which the dictator himself was a candidate could only result in the dictator stealing victory by fraud and intimidation. This, of course, is exactly what Marcos did.

What was not foreseen, however, was that the scandalously open fraudulence, reported to the world by the international press and attested to by foreign observers, including a U.S. official mission headed by Sen. Richard Lugar, would thrust the momentum which had originated with the Aquino assassination into a monumental climax in the decisive events of February 22–25 that produced the final fall of the dictatorship.

When the Batasang Pambansa, the national assembly dominated by the New Society Party (KBL), Marcos' own personal following, barefacedly proclaimed Marcos the winner, Corazon Aquino, whom Marcos had dismissed as "just an inexperienced housewife who should be confined to the bedroom," displaying superb composure and determined leadership, called for a nonviolent campaign of strikes and boycotts. Thus far she had been successful in keeping the escalating confrontation bloodless, but there was no indication of an early resolution since the Armed Forces, in spite of a reformist officers' movement, appeared still to be solidly behind Marcos. To strengthen his hold on the military, Marcos announced General Ver's retirement and named Gen. Fidel Ramos acting chief of staff on February 16.

However, on February 22, General Ramos and the defense minister, Juan Ponce Enrile, claiming they were about to be arrested by Marcos and Ver loyalists, seized the Armed Forces headquarters at Camp Aguinaldo and, across the Epifanio de los Santos Avenue (EDSA), the constabulary headquarters at

Camp Crame. They later consolidated their positions at Crame, with the support of an estimated 400 men, and telephoned Cardinal Jaime L. Sin, the archbishop of Manila, for help. The cardinal (as well as Agapito "Butz" Aquino, the martyr's brother) immediately issued a call to the faithful and citizens of metropolitan Manila to surround the camp and keep the Marcos-Ver forces from reaching the rebels. One of the most effective lines of communication was Radio Veritas, the Catholic station, the transmitter of which was later to be bombed by loyalists.

It was at this point that "people power" reached its historic high point. Priests, nuns, and ordinary faithful fingering rosaries and wielding roses knelt in front of tanks, offered the tank commanders sandwiches, reminding them that everyone at EDSA (and there were an estimated 2 million of them) was their brother and sister. The tanks and soldiers retreated, and gradually the embattled Enrile and Ramos gained the allegiance of the bulk of the Armed Forces.

The isolated dictator found himself with no alternative but to accept the offer of the U.S. Government to fly him, his family, and some of his cronies out of Malacanang Palace by helicopters to Clark Air Base in Central Luzon, and eventually to Guam and Hickam Air Base in Hawaii.

On February 19, three days before the EDSA/Crame revolution, the U.S. Senate, in a vote of eighty-five to nine, had declared the Philippine elections "marred by widespread fraud." On February 20, the House Foreign Affairs Committee also had voted unanimously to halt direct U.S. aid to the Philippines. These actions, together with the strong pronouncements against the frauds by Senator Lugar and the members of his mission, while they were still in the Philippines, ought to have been enough to elicit some appreciative Philippine feelings.

However, President Reagan confuted it all with his own contradicting and vacillating signals. After categorically blaming Marcos for "widespread fraud and violence," he retreated and attempted to blame "both sides" for the cheating, hastening to offer the hilarious explanation that, after all, "they have a two-party system there." The residual taste left in the mouth was one of resentment and suspicion that the Americans "as usual" were trying to take credit for events which the U.S. Government, after all, had effectively delayed by stubbornly and officially supporting the dictatorship.

The love-hate relationship between the Filipinos and Americans is back in the news with a vengeance, and it probably will never fade away. In 1898, the Aguinaldo republic had defeated the forces of Imperial Spain. In turn, after a bloody four-year war, the United States defeated Aguinaldo and hastily put together a colonial policy that, in its ambivalence, was to reflect the raging domestic debate between the imperialists and the anti-imperialists, the precursors of the doves and hawks of the great Vietnam War debate.

To please the imperialists, the Philippines were converted into a U.S. economic vassal, the way the British treated India, the French Indochina, and the Dutch Indonesia. However, to please the anti-imperialists the Filipinos were extended a measure of political autonomy and personal freedom superior to that given to any colonial people perhaps in the whole of human history. Philippine recognition of this concession produced the so-called "special relations" between the United States and the Philippines, which reached an emotional climax in the joint "Fil-American" campaign in the Pacific War, capped by the redemption of the MacArthur pledge of "I shall return!"

However, the post-martial-law Filipinos, having experienced thirteen years of U.S.-supported repression, have begun to sort out the fine features of the image which they have thus far fantasized about America. True, the lines at the U.S. Consulate in Manila are still long and full of Filipinos aspiring for some kind of visa to enter the United States to seek dollar-earning jobs. However, this is an economic, politically irrelevant reality, for the lines are long, too, of Filipinos seeking work in the oil fields of Saudi Arabia.

The post-martial-law Filipinos are beginning to realize that it is deceitful of anyone to tell them that, as a people, they were taught democracy by strangers. America, indeed, passed on to us extremely valuable forms, electoral rules, and legislative institutions with which to give shape to the original consensual and participatory democracy which, as the following pages will relate, we already were practicing before the advent of Western colonialism, simultaneously with some of our Asian neighbors.

At EDSA/Crame, those millions of peaceful Filipino revolutionaries did not confront the tank commanders with Jeffersonian and Lincolnian slogans, although they were certainly taught enough of those in school. The tank commanders were made, instead, to listen to prayers, "Our Fathers," "Hail Marys" and "Glory Bes," which the Philippine public school system, originally organized by Americans, had banned from the classrooms. When the revolutionaries needed a visible symbol around which to rally, they did not bring out statues of Jefferson or Lincoln, or of the nineteenth-century Filipino martyr José Rizal, or of the slain twentieth-century national hero Benigno Aquino, Jr. (although his favorite yellow color was everywhere prevailing). They brought out, instead, an image of the Blessed Virgin Mary, for when a man is ready to stand to the death for freedom, his first thought is to return to his fundamental faith. It was the miscalculation of the American colonizer in the Philippines that a person's education should be separated from his faith, that democracy is best practiced when public institutions are independent, nay, defiant, of the religion of the people.

This was a principle that was valid, indeed necessary, in the context of America, for the original European settlers in the New World were, in fact, refugees from political and religious persecution—Protestants escaping from Catholics, Catholics escaping from Protestants, Protestants escaping from fellow Protestants. The only way America could survive was to build a wall of separation of church from state. However, the American view of church and state is, obviously, only one of several working perspectives in the world. The democratic northern European peoples of today are quite comfortable with their constitutional monarchs who are also heads of the state religion but whose governments cooperate, not do battle, with established religions of all denominations.

The original Malays who settled the Philippines were not escaping any religious repression. They were practitioners of a passive religion called animism and were readily converted first when Islam came to their south and then Catholicism to their central and northern islands. Islam and Catholicism became part of their national identity. Religion was something to be embraced and lived passionately, not something to be gingerly placed on some shelf for casual examination.

The Filipino Muslims saw the marriage of religion and civics worth defending with their lives, and the U.S. Army had to invent the .45 caliber pistol to stop the determined Moro combatant in his tracks. The U.S. Government also made a different kind of war on the Filipino Catholic. It tried to separate him from his faith by forbidding its practice in public schools maintained with his tax money.

What happened at EDSA/Crame was that it was as if some booming voice from nowhere (some would say from heaven) had demanded "Will the real Filipinos please stand up and be recognized?" The real Filipinos, indeed, stood up and turned out to be native lovers of freedom and equality, believers in the practice of popular choice, i.e., democracy. Their decision to opt for the image of the Blessed Virgin Mary to rally 'round and strengthen their final resolve to regain their liberties obviously transcended their Jeffersonian education, but it did not contradict it.

On the contrary, when the revolutionaries emotionally confirmed their belief that the Son of the Virgin was a just God who made all Filipinos, and all men, deserving of freedom from tyranny, they were, in fact, paraphrasing Jefferson, who had written not that all men had evolved equal, but that they had all been created equal. It is the indiscriminate application of scientific evolutionary theories, with their pitfalls of "natural selection" and "stages of development," that forms the basis of imperialist crusades and right-wing racism. Like the Reverend Josiah Strong, who delivered sermons in the mid-nineteenth century sanctifying American manifest destiny, and poet Rudyard Kipling, whose rhyming exhortation to Americans to "take up the White Man's burden" in the Philippines sometimes has been mistaken to have been addressed to the British in India, there are still tribal groupings in the twentieth century, like the Afrikaners of South Africa, who continue to believe in a mission to dominate and repress inferior races until they are able to evolve into a stage of development deserving political equality.

There was another level of extremism that was isolated by the revolutionaries—that of the Left. The romantic visions of Lenin and later of Mao have been thought to appeal compellingly to many sectors of the Philippine population since the Pacific War, but at EDSA/Crame the adherents of those visions were not much in evidence. They had opted to exclude themselves from the "action," and even if they had not, it was evident from the mood of the revolution that any red banners would have been overwhelmed by the yellow standards of Corazon Aquino.

The troubles and disillusionments of the Left, of course, had begun many years before, with the Soviet moves into Czechoslovakia, Hungary, Poland, and later Afghanistan. Mao Tsetung's headstrong plunges had to be reversed by his successors to avert disaster in China. In December, 1985, I called on Chinese President Li Xiannian in Beijing with a Christian Democratic International delegation. He spent almost two hours explaining that Mao had been a good man but had "made many mistakes."

The blame for the "Great Leap Forward" Mao "shared with others," but the blame for the "cultural revolution" was Mao's alone, President Li asserted. We saw all over China how the new leadership was trying to recover from the monstrous and bloody errors of Maoism by reintroducing into the society increasing measures of the original dynamism of the Chinese individual. The vision of Mao appears to have been permanently rejected in his own native China. Now his country is being moved into a sort of socialism with individual dignity and initiative. The obverse of that vision, an almost identical "other side of the coin," as it were, namely, individual dignity with social responsibility, is the very vision that Christian Democrats, as well as other persuasions in the pluralist spectrum, such as the social democrats and the liberals, would like to pursue in a democracy, without the excesses and massive decapitations occasioned by the practice of scientific socialism.

A distinguished refugee from those excesses, Vietnamese intellectual Tran Van Dinh summed up the meaning of the achievement of the Filipino revolution of February, 1986, in a telegram he addressed to me a few days after the victory. Recalling that John F. Kennedy, impressed with the staunch West German commitment to democracy in the face of the Berlin Wall, had been moved to declare *"Ich bin ein Berliner,"* Dr. Tran now wrote, "Henceforth all who are continuing to struggle for freedom, justice, and democracy can proudly say, 'I am a Filipino!' "

At the very least, the revolution reminded the world that for the Filipino, democracy is not a borrowed, not an imported, not a transplanted, but an indigenous value. In its transcendence, it also broadly hinted that democracy is a value that is native to all races of humankind. The consequence is, as American poet Archibald MacLeish put it, "Democracy is the only valid revolution today." The following pages will attempt to document this truth.

Raul S. Manglapus
Makati, Philippines
May 15, 1986

Acknowledgments

This book was written to investigate a political exile's suspicion that his yearnings for democratic freedoms were not just an idiosyncrasy of his race, but a sentiment universal in all cultures, Western and non-Western alike. Therefore, encouragement came mainly from those committed to the daily monitoring and sustaining of this universal sentiment, men and women from disparate positions within the democratic spectrum.

The grant for this investigation reached me through Freedom House in New York, whose director, Leonard Sussman, was the principal mover behind its publication. Raymond Gastil, editor of Freedom House's annual survey on political rights and civil liberties in the world, provided me with guidelines for analytical objectivity.

Lindsay Mattison and Virginia Foote, director and assistant director, respectively, at the International Center for Development Policy in Washington, D.C., where I was serving as president while doing this study, saw to it that I was afforded the time to do it as well as the insights by which to distinguish sham from reality in democracy.

Michael Horowitz, director of the Institute for Development Anthropology in Binghamton, N.Y., was responsible for putting together for me a plan to scan early cultures to detect democratic toleration of deviants.

Dick Ruffin, Washington director, and R.D. Mathur, Indian trustee of Moral Re-Armament or MRA (a movement whose dedication to pluralism in society is as important as its drive for social morality) opened doors for me to the village managers in Eastern India and experts on community life among the Indian hill peoples. H. G. Elliott, the English civil servant, whose specially prepared report on Nigerian democracy I quote in full, is also with MRA. In the Indian Karnataka State it was the distinguished journalist C. G. K. Reddy who introduced me to leaders of the *panchayats*—indigenous village governments—based in Bangalore.

My Christian Democratic colleagues in Ecuador recommended me to their Ministry of Education and Culture, facilitating my access to the Otavalos, Shuaras and Saraguros, descendants of the original peoples on the fringes of the Incan empire.

Fayetta de Montigny, former assistant executive director of the National Advisory Council on Indian Education in Washington, D.C., opened doors for me to her Seneca-Cayuga tribe in Oklahoma, while Professor Robert Young of the University of New Mexico in Albuquerque introduced me to the Navajos.

Paul Ssemogerere, leader of the Bugandans and the Democratic Party of Uganda, guided me to personal glimpses of East African indigenous practices, with which Asmarom Legesse, the Ethiopian anthropologist from Swarthmore College in Pennsylvania, had already acquainted me in a lengthy personal interview.

The strongest ideological support for this study came from the Democracy International, that unique gathering of exiles from both left- and right-wing dictatorships, based in Washington, D.C., who have united to dramatize their preference for pluralist democracy and their rejection of the extremes of intolerance and repression that prevail in their countries.

And I must not forget my generous daughter-in-law Ria, who obligingly retyped the whole manuscript in double-space when my word processing module would not work.

Introduction

"What is Jazz?", someone asked the late pianist Fats Waller. "If you have to ask," he replied, "you'll never know!"

Is it necessary to ask, "What is democracy?" Who will respond? Who is qualified to tell when a society is democratic? The historian? The political scientist? The anthropologist? The philosopher? They all are qualified, but only they?

Plato taught that all men are endowed with *Politike techne*, the art of political judgment. Any human being can tell when he is free, when his community is free, when his country is free. Yet, Plato himself mistrusted this universal art in its free exercise, i.e., democracy. Along with Aristotle, he attacked other Greeks, like Protagoras, who dared to develop democratic theory.

No one knows of Protagoras today except through a minute reading of Plato and Socrates, who both exchanged parodies about him. The Greeks as a people never developed their own theory of democracy, but that did not matter. As American classicist Moses I. Finley stated, "The [Greek] philosophers attacked democracy; the committed democrats responded by ignoring them, by going about the business of government and politics in a democratic way, without writing treatises on the subject." (Moses I. Finley, *Democracy Ancient and Modern*. New Brunswick, N.J.: Rutgers University Press, 1975, p. 10.)

The people of Greece rejected, too, the notion that formal

schooling is a condition precedent for the proper practice of democracy.

A young man was educated by attending the Assembly, he learned, not necessarily the size of the island of Sicily (a purely technical question, as both Protagoras and Socrates would have agreed), but the political issues facing Athens, the choices, the arguments, and he learned to assess the men who put themselves forward as policymakers, as leaders. (Finley, p. 12.)

Uninfluenced by the Greek model but simultaneous with it, other European cultures developed their own participatory mechanisms. The Romans recorded witnessing Teutonic assemblies called *ding*, which "all men fit to fight" were required to attend for prolonged discussions which concluded with unanimous decisions arrived at by consensus. No formal schooling was required for attendance, there being no formal schools available.

In my country, the extension of the vote to the "illiterate" Filipino farmer was once vigorously resisted by theoreticians who feared he was not "prepared" for democracy, but leaders like Jeremias Montemayor of the Federation of Free Farmers convincingly asked, "Who knows better of the problems of the farmer than the farmer himself?"

The best, the only education for democracy is democracy itself. If so, it should be self-evident that all cultures, if they have not yet practiced democracy, deserve to do so. This means that democracy could have been the natural state of human beings in many cultures, Western and non-Western as well. This also means that there is more to democracy than form, i.e., efficient bureaucracy, parliamentary rules. There is substance—the condition of a society which respects the community and the individual, restrains arbitrariness, tolerates dissent. The most visible mark of this condition is the ability of the individual to be an active rather than a passive component of the community and, therefore, to participate in its decision-making process.

In my years of exile from the dictatorship that replaced Philippine democracy, I have had repeatedly to field the questions

"Was your country really ready for democracy?" and "Is not democracy a purely Western experience?" Who is qualified to respond to these questions? All of us, because we possess the art of political judgment. I also have my modest credentials as one who has had his share of studying and practicing the democratic arts. Happily, I need not stand on that experience alone. In making this study, I only needed to organize bountiful extant material depicting the global performance of original democracy. In the last two years, I also managed to visit representative areas in Asia, Latin America, Africa, and indigenous United States.

It is my hope that, after reading this study, one might quietly exclaim in paraphrase of Winston Churchill's classic epigram: "Democracy has been the least practiced of all forms of government—except for all the others!"

Will of the People

1 Democracy and Despotism: Chicken and Egg?

A perennial American cartoon show favorite for children and adults alike is "The Flintstones." It seems almost never to fail to entertain because of its barefaced, not too subtle anachronism—two prehistoric families, living next door to each other, the men clad in prehistoric animal skins, driving to office in stone-wheeled automobiles, watching stone-framed television sets, keeping baby dinosaurs for pets instead of Irish Setters.

Behind the apparently ingenuous anachronism of rock-carved vehicles and television screens, however, is a far more subtle one, a sociohistorical incongruity which might perhaps better account for the cartoon's seemingly unending comic appeal. Those prehistoric characters, in the popular and conventional understanding, should not only be seen living in bare caves, instead of in furnished albeit "petrified" homes, but the husbands should also be sketched as clubbing their wives on the head and dragging them around by their hair instead of meekly accompanying them shopping or having to conjure up clever excuses for stealing away from them for a game of poker with the boys. Each family ought also to be uncomfortably perceived as in a perpetual state of paternal despotism and interfamily relations as in permanent tension.

Instead, viewers may relax and enjoy watching the two neighboring households as they engage with comforting regularity in happy, riotous outings and unerringly find ways of concluding intra- and interfamily misunderstandings in tearful reconciliations. In brief, the Flintstone family and their neighbors are faltering but successful practitioners of mutual respect, as ordinary, red-blooded, twentieth-century, democratic, American human beings are wont to be.

It is this monstrous incongruity that makes the cartoon so irresistibly funny and entertaining, for the myth of the intolerant, club-wielding, women-by-the-hair-dragging caveman dies hard. Defending discrimination against women in a Washington, D.C., golf club, a *Time* reader wrote to the editor in October, 1984: "I wish someone would explain why women insist on corrupting male-only establishments... prehistoric man dealt with women's liberation quite well with his club." (*Time*, October 22, 1984, p. 6.)

"The Flintstones," then, is an immensely successful travesty because its proposition is simple and so widely accepted: prehistoric human beings could not have been either so civilized or so democratic. This study begins by disputing that proposition. "The Flintstones" is not just a successful travesty. It is an historical blunder.

For years we have known of the discovery of delicately limned, richly hued paintings of animals on cave walls certified to have been drawn many millennia ago by human beings of obviously high sensitivity. The paintings show an authorship differing from the apes not in degree but in kind—civilized, if you will, even when judged by the most up-to-date space-age criteria, for if art is the mark of civilization, then when the "primitive" caveman first appeared upon the earth he, without waiting for centuries of "development," could have justly laid claim to being unqualifiedly civilized. On the other hand, the evidence on club-wielding and hair-pulling has always been nil. The notion has always been of the stuff of whimsical legend, perhaps reinforced by the theory that man is descended from the ape—although even the ape has never been established scientifically as being inevitably or even compulsively a despot among its kind.

All this speculation on the despotic caveman could be dismissed as pure, if entertaining, intellectual exercise did it not provide the very first debating premise for modern policy propositions on the universality of democratic values. The Flintstones, in settling differences among themselves and with their neighbors, sometimes angrily but always with ultimate mutual respect, were, in fact, practicing the substance of democracy in its dictionary definition of "a social condition of equality and respect for the individual in the community." (*American Heritage Dictionary*, 1975 ed., p. 351.)

However, if the caricatured anachronism is the cruel truth, i.e., if, indeed, the cartoon is genuinely comical because primitive human beings could not have possibly behaved the way the Flintstones do but could arrive at decisions only by club-swinging males dictating the terms, then we are dangerously close to proving that democracy as a substantial value—and its collective sister value, human rights—indeed may be said not to have been part of the natural state of humankind. In addition, if the original human beings and human communities were devoid of these values, then we are suddenly confronted with a deceptively solid justification for all those bloody, mostly one-sided slaughtering wars of "civilizing conquest."

Furthermore, if democratic equality can only be possible with sophisticated historical evolution, then the unpredictable course of history could cause democracy to evolve exclusively, or at least much earlier, in certain areas of the world, for example, Western Europe, while the rest of the human population develops in despotism. This would then provide "historical" rationalizations for all forms of dictatorship and formidable excuses for internal Western support for repression in developing countries as a "necessary" stage in the development toward "ultimate" democracy.

Yet, as we shall see in subsequent chapters, the historical and anthropological evidence tends to demonstrate the reverse process. The first human communities were democratic societies, not in the complex modern parliamentary form but, as G. K. Chesterton puts it, "peasants tilling patches of their own land in a rough equality, and meeting to vote directly under a village tree,... the most truly self-governing of men." Even for the most passionate Darwinian evolutionist, Chesterton wryly suggests, there should be "really no reason why men should not have had at least as much camaraderie as rats or rooks."

(G. K. Chesterton, *The Everlasting Man*. Garden City, N.Y.: Image Books, 1955, p. 61.)

Lewis H. Morgan, in his seminal 1877 work *Ancient Society*, traces the development of civilization from the original *gens* ("a body of consanguinei descended from a common ancestor"), to a *phratry* ("an organic association of two or more *gentes*"), to a tribe ("composed of several *gentes*, developed from two or more *phratry*, all the members of which are intermingled by marriage, and all of whom speak the same dialect"), to developed confederacies, nations, or states. (Lewis H. Morgan, *Ancient Society*. Cambridge: Belknap Press reprint, 1964.) Morgan asserted:

> It was impossible for a kingdom to arise by natural growth in any part of the earth under gentile institutions. I venture to make this suggestion at this early stage of the discussion in order to call attention more closely to the structure and principles of ancient society, as organized in *gentes, phratries,* and tribes. Monarchy is incompatible with gentilism. It belongs to a latter period of civilization. (Morgan, p. 35.)

Morgan concedes that "despotisms appeared in some instances among the Grecian tribes in the upper status of barbarism," but these despotisms, he asserts,

> were founded upon usurpation, were considered illegitimate by the people, and were, in fact, alien to the ideas of gentile society. The Grecian tyrannies were despotisms founded upon usurpation and were the germ out of which the later kingdoms arose; while the so-called kingdoms of the heroic age were military democracies, and nothing more. (Morgan, p. 111.)

It is relevant to note that Morgan chose to make these observations not in connection with European societies but in his chapters on the Iroquois tribes and confederacy, which we shall view more closely later.

Even in the recorded history of the Romanization of Europe, democracy preceded despotism. The early Teutonic *Volksversammlung*, or people's assemblies referred to as *Thing* (a name which survives in the modern legislative bodies of Norway as

Storting, in Denmark as *Folketing*, and in Iceland as *Alting*) ultimately were abolished by the conquering Romans, permitting the rise to power of absolutist kings and dukes. (Joseph Kasule, "Palaver and Its Influence in Current Constitutional and International Law." Ph.D diss., University of Cologne, 1972, pp. 25–28.)

Earlier elsewhere, as scattered villages got coerced together by a central government that was successful, as in Egypt, in establishing tight communications, the original democracy likewise disappeared, yielding to despotism at the center. However, we shall see that in regions where the construction of communications was not so successful, as in China, the original democracy persisted in spite of fabled imperial splendor at the capital. Sometimes, it may not have taken a successful centralized despotism to destroy the original democracy. Sometimes, as Chesterton again so aptly states, "as fatigue falls on a community, the citizens are less inclined for that eternal vigilance which has truly been called the price of liberty...a despotism may almost be defined as tired democracy." (Chesterton, p. 60.)

Throughout human history we shall see despotism and democracy coexist in many parts of the world, but what Morgan is saying is that democracy came first and despotism later. Democracy was then the natural state of humankind. The point where "archaeology [prehistory] merges with documentary history" is about 3000 B.C., when the Babylonians developed their cuneiform characters. (Elman R. Service, *Origins of the State and Civilization*. New York: Norton, 1975, p. 25.) Thus, the dawn of recorded human history finds humankind already civilized and, as we shall later see, democratic. On the other hand, even archaeology has not uncovered any conclusive evidence of a despotic "caveman civilization," and "the despotism in certain dingy and decayed tribes in the twentieth century does not prove that the first men were ruled despotically. It does not even suggest it; it does not even begin to hint at it." (Chesterton, p. 60.)

Despite the evidence, authors with impressive credentials have contributed regrettably to the notion that despotism is the natural non-Western way of life. Referring mostly to the civilizations of the Near East, India, and China, Karl Wittfogel asserts that "the common substance in the various Oriental societies appeared most conspicuously in the despotic strength of their political authority." Wittfogel gracefully concedes, "Of course, tyrannical governments were not unknown in Europe." "But," he adds, "critical observers saw that Eastern absolutism was definitely more comprehensive and more oppressive than its Western counterpart. To them, 'Oriental' despotism presented the harshest form of power." He recalls that even Montesquieu was "primarily concerned with the distressing personal effects of Oriental despotism." (Karl Wittfogel, *Oriental Despotism*. New Haven: Yale University Press, 1957, pp. 11–13.)

Wittfogel builds his case on a theoretically solid foundation—the historically certifiable tradition that the world's civilizations invariably have begun around sources of water. He then conceptualizes the "hydraulic society," whose structure and institutions are shaped by the compulsive need to tap, distribute, and utilize water sources for sustenance, irrigation, and transportation. In the rice culture, which dominated Asia, the peculiarities in the process of cultivating the grain required "orderly cooperation" and "planned integration," which, inevitably, it is argued, led to bureaucratic landlordism, a bureaucratic capitalism, and a bureaucratic gentry supporting an absolutist monarchy at the top. The argument is applied to explain despotism in the hydraulic societies of China, India, Turkestan, Mesopotamia, Egypt, and Meso-America.

Did these hydraulic despots rule in the space-computer age there could be less doubting the validity of the Wittfogel theory. With such absolute power at the center and with computerized communications at one's pushbutton command, the remotest village could be under the total control—mercy, if you will—of the reigning despot. However, Wittfogel's model Oriental despots did not live in this age but in times of primitive communications.

The late Jesuit historian Horacio de la Costa used to remind me that whether in Europe, Asia, or Africa, a monarch in those days, being satisfied with enough tribute and sometimes with enough concubines, would leave the local communities in his realm alone to govern themselves from day to day. Even if he had wanted to interfere, in most cases, he could not have because of primitive communications.

Will Durant confirms this in the Chinese context:

> The great distances that separated one [Chinese] city from another and all of them from the imperial capital, the dividing effect of mountains, deserts, and unbridged or unnavigable streams, the lack of transport and quick communications, and the difficulty of supporting an army large enough to enforce some central will upon four hundred million people, compelled the state to leave to each district an almost complete autonomy. (Will Durant, *The Story of Civilization, Part I: Our Oriental Heritage.* New York: Simon and Schuster, 1954, pp. 796–97.)

State officials were, indeed, appointed for local administration, "but these officials normally contented themselves with collecting taxes and 'squeezes,' judging such cases as voluntary arbitration had failed to settle, and, for the rest, leaving the maintenance of order to custom, the family, the clan and the guild." Durant continues, "Each province was a semi-independent state, free from imperial interference or central legislation so long as it paid its tax allotment and kept the peace." The communications problem had its impact even on the quality of Chinese patriotism. "Lack of facilities of communication made the central government more an idea than a reality. The patriotic emotions of the people were spent upon their districts and provinces, and seldom extended to the empire as a whole." (Durant, pp. 796–97.)

"It is evident," writes Service, "that the Chou dynasty cannot have ruled a centralized empire containing such diverse regions, inhabited by communities developing at different rates of growth." The Chinese emperor, Service concludes, "was at the center of a culture rather than a government." (Service, pp. 255–56.)

The respected, though perhaps understandably less unbiased Chinese republican patriot Sun Yat-sen recalls that "apart from paying the regular grain taxes, the [Chinese] people had almost no relation with the officials." Again, "The people had little direct relation to the emperor beyond paying him the annual grain tax—nothing more." Blaming the sufferings of his people more on foreign political and economic domination than on domestic tyranny, Sun asserted that "the Chinese people have not been subject to the oppression of the autocracy . . . [and] therefore, felt very little resentment against their emperors." Wittfogel's blanket indictment of Eastern absolutism as "definitely more comprehensive and more oppressive than its Western counterpart" is sharply turned around by Sun, who contrasts the lack of direct oppression of the people by the Chinese autocracy with "the autocracy of Europe [which] was quite different from China." Sun pointed out that "the despotism in Europe, from the downfall of Rome up to two or three centuries ago, had been developing rapidly and the people had suffered increasingly and unbearably. Europeans indeed suffered 'deep waters and burning fires' from the denial of freedom," Sun wrote. That is how, in his view, it was in Europe that lasting revolutionary ideas were born. "So, whenever they [the Europeans] heard of anyone leading a struggle for liberty, they all rejoiced and espoused his cause. Such was the beginning of the European revolutionary idea." (Sun Yat-sen, *The Principle of Democracy*. Westport, Conn.: Greenwood Press, reprint, 1970, pp. 28–31.)

What took place then in the virtually unreachable villages of China is discussed in a later chapter, but the Chinese model is here sorted out in advance because it has come to be regarded in undiscriminating circles as the epitome of Oriental despotism. And we shall see that the phenomenon of an ostensibly omnipotent central government forced to accept extended local autonomy in the far reaches of the realm has not been unique to China but has been mostly an historical invariable in all early civilizations.

This valuable and readily available basic political information has not impressed, or may not have come to the attention of, influential Western authors, including Americans, who continue to proclaim a Western monopoly of the original democratic ideal. Whether unintentionally or by design, their claims, bordering on the condescending, are premised on a confusion of form with substance. For instance, George F. Kennan avers that he knows "of no evidence that 'democracy' or what we picture to ourselves under that word, is the natural state of most of mankind." He suggests,

> It seems rather to be a form of government (and a difficult one, with many drawbacks, at that) which evolved in the eighteenth and nineteenth centuries in northwestern Europe, primarily among those countries that border on the English Channel and the North Sea (but with a certain extension into Central Europe), and which was then carried into other parts of the world, including North America, where peoples from that northwestern Europe area appeared as original settlers, or a colonialists, and had laid down the prevailing patterns of civil government. (George F. Kennan, *The Cloud of Danger: Current Realities of American Foreign Policy*, excerpted in the *Washington Post*, July 1, 1977, op-ed page.)

Not bothering to distinguish between form and substance, Kennan then feels entitled to conclude that "democracy has, in other words, a relatively narrow base in time and in space," and, dismissing the volumes of probatory material in public libraries, laments that "the evidence has yet to be produced that [democracy] is the natural form of rule for peoples outside of those narrow perimeters." (Kennan, ibid.) Note that Kennan, in referring to the same conceptualization of democracy, interchangeably uses "natural form" and "natural state," the latter connoting not just a formal but a substantial condition of the society.

William F. Buckley, Jr., displays, although rather more predictably, the same disdain for these useful distinctions. Defending Asian "authoritarian" regimes, he proceeds, with accustomed lexical agility, to make his own distinction "between political rights (which are a luxury of orderly disciplined people) and human rights (which are a metaphysical patrimony)." He laments the tendency in activist rhetoric "to use a word 'democracy' as a rough substitute for civic virtue," implying that all these concepts are beyond comprehension by the Oriental mind, and accepting at face value the self-serving assertion by the deputy prime minister in the dictatorial government of South Korea that "there is not one developing country in the world where Western democracy really works."

(William F. Buckley, Jr., "Can Developing Countries Be Democratic?" The *Washington Star*, June 7, 1977, op-ed page.)

Even more predictably, William Randolph Hearst, Jr., in one of his Sunday columns in the *San Francisco Examiner* in 1976, would deny that there is any "such thing as a right—in the American sense—in any Oriental language, and since all that anyone can be in the view of the average person in the Orient is the role assigned to him by religion and society, there can only be duties—not 'rights!' "

This should be startling news to Indonesians, Malaysians, Urdu, Punjabi, and Persians, who use the Arabic word *haqq*; the Hindi and Bengali who have their *adhikar* and the Sanskrit *svetve*; the Thais their *sitthi*; the Koreans their *kooanri*; and the Filipinos their *karapatan*—all mean "rights." The ideographic characters for the Chinese words *ren ch'uan* and the Japanese *jin ken* are identical, and they both denote human rights.

Clare Boothe Luce would venture further in the field of speculative condescension and indulge in gratuitous statistics. "Three quarters of the nations of the world," she states quite categorically, "are not culturally adapted to democracy." Her disdain for the penchant of some Americans to, as Kennan decries it, "impose their own [democratic] values, traditions, and habits of thought on people for whom these things have no validity and no usefulness" leads her somewhat irrationally to reject even humanitarian appeals to international compassion. Scoffing at "pictures in the papers of a starving mother [in some developing country] with her child holding out its hand," she snorts: "I would feel a little more compassion if one of my pet birds had a broken leg in its cage in my own house." (Clare Boothe Luce, interview in *Geo Magazine*, March 1980.)

The Flintstones blunder has found the ultimate believer.

2 Marx and Toynbee *vs.* the "Cake of Custom"

Some political scientists, journalists and activists may perhaps be absolved for not conceding to the original consensual traditions of humankind its proper role in the dynamics of the eternal struggle for human improvement. It is the philosophers of history, with their sweeping and apocalyptic views of the human experience, who must accept responsibility for this costly omission, for historians like to analyze the march of events mostly in terms of clashes between kingdoms, dynasties, empires, civilizations—and their rise and fall. Apocalyptic thinkers direct their anxieties toward conflicts between social classes. Neither will much remember the reality at the bottom, the foundation of civilization—the local, popular community. Some, in fact, would dismiss it as part of the problem, prescribing its total absorption into centralized urbanization as the first step to "modernization."

For Arnold Toynbee, who acquired his initial perceptions of global realities at the British Archaeological School in Athens, the proper unit of historical study was not the local community, not even the traditional unit, the nation-state, but a civilization. He shared with Karl Marx, whose view from the British Museum focused on world classes, a common obsession with the "proletariat." Toynbee perceived the whole of human history as a series of challenges and responses. In each instance, he saw a "creative minority," generally mystically inspired, providing leadership to a "passive majority" which voluntarily accepts the minority's solutions. But to unify a universal state, force becomes necessary; the minority becomes dominant rather than creative, stimulating the growth of an "external and internal proletariat," contained by force rather than acceptance. The reaction to this force from both sectors of the proletariat produces a new civilization.

Marx's proletariat was the victim of social injustice that he saw meted out by the British Industrial Revolution mostly in the slums of early nineteenth century London. He detected in the apparently helpless slum dwellers conclusive proof that man's mind and will cannot determine the shape of social institutions. This function could only be performed by the relationships of the forces of production. To achieve a just society, the victimized participants in the relationship—the proletariat—must rise, seize political power, and change the relationship forever.

Neither Toynbee nor Marx bothered to investigate the natural state of man before the proletariat—the Roman, in Toynbee's retrospect, and the British in Marx's—ever came into existence. Neither of them, nor any of their peers in historiography, ever bothered to wonder whether one valid perspective, analysis, or explanation, if you will, of the human condition might be the continuing tension between democracy at the base and autocracy at the top, between consensual tradition and institutionalized law, between a natural condition of freedom and an internally or externally imposed artificial repression. The result of this failure has been the application to indigenous problems of solutions drawn from alien experiences.

"Part of the trouble," writes anthropologist Service, "in interpreting the Marxian scheme arises from the theoretical confusion of trying to make universal stages out of particular historical sequences." He points out that a uniquely European historical sequence, "the Roman Empire and the political decentralization, power vacuum, and local economic self-sufficiency that prevailed after its fall," was elevated to a sequence of universal stages. This error, says Service, led to two important problems. First, it caused "insuperable difficulties in attempts to adapt Marxist thought to the cultural evolution of the world." As we shall see later in the chapter on the Aztecs, the Spanish conquistadores were guilty of the same naivete in evaluating what they perceived as a strange new civilization in traditional European feudalistic terms. The second problem is "that in terms of European history in particular, the evolutionary significance of the primary archaic civilization is needlessly downgraded and feudalism elevated to a stage that it never was." (Elman R. Service, *Origins of the State and Civilization*. New York: Norton, 1975, p. 36.)

The error has not been confined to the Marxist end of the spectrum and could begin to explain how more moderate thinkers like Kennan can claim that democracy was not the natural, i.e., original, state of most of mankind, including most of Europe; for if democracy is a "social condition of equality and respect for the individual within the community," then the "primary archaic civilizations" were closer to democracy than to the feudalism and despotism which some would seek to generalize in both Western and non-Western historical contexts. (George F. Kennan, *The Cloud of Danger: Current Realities of American Foreign Policy*, excerpted in the *Washington Post*, July 1, 1977, op-ed page.)

"Man in a state of nature," writes Service, was "the egalitarian society." This social condition was a sort of absurd democracy, where there was equality without formal government, and leadership was sporadic, acquired by charisma rather than by force. The ethic of equality was so strong that the ideal personality was self-effacing, a fact which was partly responsible for the impermanence of leadership.

Jesuit Father LeJeune observed of the primitive Montaignais-Naskapi of Labrador in 1634 that the individual Indian will "not endure in the least those who seem desirous of assuming superiority over others." (Service, p. 36.) Confronted with this "self-effacement in leadership," how was order maintained in the society? It was here that customary law began, not codified or formalized but more in the form of, as anthropologists Walter Bagehot and Sidney Hartland would suggest, the "cake of custom," the "power of cultural norms over the individuality of persons." The power of custom precluded the need for force and provided enough informal means of preserving order, rendering formal government unnecessary. In the absence of a permanent authority, when disputes arose, the public mediated. Unanimity of consensus was sought, and to resolve doubts, public duels or contests between the disputants were allowed. Absolute vindication ("an eye for an eye") was not required. Certainly the taking of a life for the loss of another was not the rule, partly perhaps because of the lack of a formal authority to issue the death sentence but obviously due also to the egalitarian principle of respect for the individual.

One of the contemporary societies that has preserved its original egalitarianism is that of the Eskimos, among whom rank and class are so thoroughly absent that, Kaj Birket-Smith notes with wry anthropologist's humor, they "therefore must renounce that satisfaction, which Thackeray calls the true pleasure of life, of associating with one's inferiors!" (Kaj Birket-Smith, *The Eskimos*. London: Methuen & Co., Ltd., 1936, p. 144.) An East Greenlander Eskimo may seek satisfaction through a song contest (instead of other permitted forms like wrestling and head-butting) "if he is physically too weak to gain his end, or if he is so skilled in singing as to feel certain of victory." The successful rationale for the singing duel, which is carried on at some length to give the public time to form unanimity of consensus, is that the "East Greenlanders get so engrossed in the mere artistry of singing as to forget the cause of the grudge." (Service, p. 57.)

If this sounds amiably absurd, it is at least indicative of that quality of an egalitarian society which puts it closer to democracy than despotism, the underplaying of the vindictive aspect of the administration of justice. Even if it may be irrelevant to the question of guilt (as are other methods of dispute settlement in other egalitarian societies such as the distance spear-throwing-dodging duel among Australian aborigines), it contrasts sharply with the far more cruel irrelevance of the trial by ordeal and the duels to the death of medieval and postmedieval Western society.

Early egalitarian societies that somehow maintained the stability of their small population persisted in their isolated ways governed by custom and tradition. Those whose populations increased, thus experiencing the need for formal government, developed hierarchical systems beginning with simple chiefdoms and sometimes growing into elaborate, monarchical states. But by the time they graduated into hierarchical status, these societies already had become firmly rooted in their cake of custom which no amount of hierarchical structuring or formal government would succeed in preempting. This resulted in the most seemingly despotic chief or monarch finding himself invariably forced to submit to consultation, counsel, even election, permitting the development of indigenous democratic institutions and justifying the suspicion, still not prevalent in the West, that the natural state of mankind, whether in the West or East, was, indeed, substantive, if not formal, democracy.

The rise of formal village government occasioned the graduation of an egalitarian community into a hierarchical society. Village chiefdoms, at times hereditary, began to take shape, acquiring the sanctioning power with which to enforce formal laws and decrees. With growth and expansion also came the division of the population into social classes, and one of the functions of lawmaking was the allocation of rights among these classes.

But throughout this whole process of chiefdom and class formation, which sometimes involved the invocation of a superhuman power to legitimize authority—resulting in theocracy—the cake of custom, consolidating the ingredients of equality and respect for the individual which characterized the original egalitarianism, provided sustenance, powerful and inexhaustible, for those who would resist repression by the institutionalized authority, at times by argument, at other times by taking up arms.

It is, in fact, this frequent dichotomy between custom and authority, this tension and at times open conflict between customary law and statutory law, this continuing struggle of the human race to assert its original democracy that was bypassed by both the radical and the conservative analyses of history by Marx and Toynbee. It was, on their part, an unfortunate and fatal omission because this struggle is far more universal in the cultures of the world than those perceived by them in the slums of London or the archaeological fields of Greece and, therefore, far more applicable in their attempts to unravel the human puzzle and offer hope to the masses of the world. In most civilizations, the village system became the basis for the state because the "basic ingredients for statehood are already present, to become formalized as necessary under conditions of external stress." (Service, p. 36.) But on whatever level of development of the society, the confrontation between the body of customs born and revered in the early egalitarian stage of the society and the formal enactments of the governing authority would provide the most reliable index for the progress of the society toward equality, justice, and freedom. Customary law ensured popular participation, sometimes even popular rule, in the hierarchical society where the principal authoritative figure was either a chief or a king. Inability to appreciate this reality has led to the erroneous conventional notion that kingdoms and chiefdoms, embodiments of absolutism, were the antithesis of popular participation or sovereignty.

Democratic participation coexisted with monarchic centralism not only in those cases where, as we have seen above, central despotic control could not reach local or regional communities because of primitive communications and difficult terrain, but even in smaller, more compact hierarchical societies.

One hundred years ago, W. M. F. Allen, an American scholar from the University of Wisconsin, quoting the Roman historian Tacitus, observed that many German nations had kings, but the "sovereign power was in the hands of the whole people, acting collectively, meeting in a general assembly at stated intervals." Quoting Julius Caesar, Allen points to German

magistrates, holding their office it would seem for life, elected by the people in their national assembly, and acting as a board of administration in the intervals between the meetings of assembly, but also having each his own district where he presides over the administration of justice [but where in each] the verdict is rendered by the people of the district in an assembly of the district. (W.M.F. Allen, "The Primitive Democracy of the Germans." Paper read at the meeting of the Wisconsin Academy of Sciences, Arts, and Letters, 1881.)

These political institutions of the early Germans were essentially democratic and paralleled those, Allen suggests, of other primitive peoples of the Indo-European family (Indo-European includes the Germanic, Celtic, Italic, Baltic, Slavic, Greek, Armenian, Hittite, Tocharian, Iranian, and Indic groups). "Most of them established a kingly office," Allen concedes, "most of them had slaves or serfs or imperfectly qualified citizens to whom they stood in the relation of a ruling aristocracy: but as a rule all authority is regarded as emanating from the body of the citizens."

Thus, democratic institutions could grow even if bounded by monarchy on one side and slavery on the other. Had this not been so, there would have been no British, no Greek, and no American democracies.

3 Mesopotamia: Earliest Formal Democracy?

In searching East and West for original democratic traditions, one need not retreat when confronted with monarchy, aristocracy, nobility, or slavery. In fact, the search must begin in the East, not the West, for it is in the East that early original egalitarian societies first developed hierarchies and blossomed into mature civilizations, clustered around life-giving sources of water which provided not only irrigation but also arteries of commerce and communication, stimulating urbanization.

In fact, the earliest such civilization, Mesopotamia, was named for its position between the two great rivers Tigris and Euphrates (Greek *mesos*, middle, and *potamos*, river). It is the earliest prototype for Wittfogel's "hydraulic society," which necessitates and produces Oriental despotic power—"total and not benevolent." Indeed the most common recollections of Mesopotamia are those of original imperial despotisms. As an obscure musical playwright put it:

> In twenty-six hundred B.C.
> It was Lugal-Zaggisi
> Who first began activities imperial
> A hundred tribes asunder
> He forced to buckle under;
> And civilization thus was born Sumerial!
> (Raul S. Manglapus, *Manifest Destiny*, musical play in-

cluded in *Philippines, Silenced Democracy*, New York: Orbis, 1976.)

However, the story of the birth of an empire, focusing on the forces that it took to weld it out of scattered communities, may not bother to look into the character of the original communities. It was, in fact, the search for steady irrigation that brought farming communities to the alluvial lowlands of the Tigris-Euphrates system around 4000 B.C. In apparent contradiction of the Wittfogel theory, there was no spontaneous growth of centralized despotism among them—only villages that "were relatively self-sufficient and politically autonomous." (Elman R. Service, *Origins of the State and Civilization*. New York: Norton, 1975, p. 20.) Five hundred years later, they developed their first cities, and still 500 years later they put together the first known system of handwriting.

At that point, Service points out, "we merge archaeology [prehistory] with documentary history. It is documentary history that tells us of life and government in the Mesopotamian cities."

A. Leo Oppenheim writes of the coexistence of two components in Mesopotamian society, in a "pattern [which] maintained its effectiveness through three millennia." First there was

the community of persons of equal status bound together by a consciousness of belonging, realized by directing their communal affairs by means of an assembly, in which, under a presiding officer, some measure of consensus was reached as it was the case in the rich and quasi-independent old cities of Babylonia. (A. Leo Oppenheim, *Ancient Mesopotamia*. Chicago: University of Chicago Press, 1964, p. 95.)

Side by side with this democratic configuration there was a second "organization of persons entirely different in structure and temperament from the community just mentioned, whose center and raison d'être was either the temple or the palace, either the household of the deity or that of the king." Here, then, we have an early instance of a kingdom, within the tight confines of its city-state where the population was within reach of the royal power, which not only tolerated but complemented an operative popular sovereignty. "The solidarity of a Mesopotamian city," observes Oppenheim, "is reflected in the absence of any status or ethnic or tribal articulation." The community of citizens "constituted as an assembly" not only administered the city under a presiding official but also made legal decisions, some of them ceremonially confirmed by the king. Its coexistence with the temple-palace system created for the Mesopotamian city "an equilibrium of forces and an overall harmony that endowed the city with the longevity which the Greek Polis could not achieve." (Oppenheim, p. 114.)

However, it is another anthropologist, Thorkild Jacobsen, who provides us with deeper, and more sanguine, insights into the democratic character of Ancient Mesopotamia. Jacobsen read a paper entitled, "Primitive Democracy in Ancient Mesopotamia" at the meeting of the American Oriental Society in Chicago in April, 1941. His "primitive democracy" is more substance than form, where "sovereignty resides in the citizens," but "the various functions of government are as yet little specialized, the power structure is loose, and the machinery for social coordination is as yet imperfectly developed." He then portrays a Mesopotamia where the classic historical confrontation between democratic and autocratic tendencies takes place. The autocratic drive was strong: "The country formed a mosaic of diminutive, self-sufficient, autonomous city-states, and in each such state one individual, the ruler, united in his hands the chief political powers: legislative, judiciary, and executive." This autocratic momentum "drove Mesopotamia forward relentlessly toward the more distant aim: centralization of power within one large area." Lugal-Zaggisi achieved this goal with his "activities imperial," followed by King Sargon and the highly organized bureaucratic state of the Third Dynasty of Ur. (See *Journal of Near Eastern Studies*, July, 1943, pp. 159ff.)

Working its way up against this autocratic downstream was the egalitarian instinct of the original society, producing seemingly anachronistic democratic institutions. In Assyria the highest judicial authority was a general assembly of all the colonists: *karum sahir rabi*—"the colony young and old"—

which could be called into session by a clerk only at the bidding of a majority of its senior members. If the clerk issued the call at the request of only one individual, he was fined ten shekels of silver! Besides discharging judicial functions, the general assembly had its political duties. For example, it could overrule objections of particular colonists to the coming of commissaries sent by the legal authorities of the mother-city Assur.

In Babylonia, where "we are very naturally struck first of all by the degree to which royal power is there in evidence" anyone had recourse directly to the king for redress, and he could delegate each case to suitable courts for decision. But alongside the king and his judicial powers stood "the Babylonian city," whose town mayor and town elders settled minor disputes and where the whole town—*Puhrum*, the "assembly"—decided important cases "according to its own local ideas of right and wrong."

To prove that the participation in the *Puhrum* and its judicial function was not limited to a favored class but was open, perhaps with some degree of compulsion, to all citizens, Jacobsen quotes a Babylonian proverb which presages modern-day counsel from stand-up comedians to potential witness summons dodgers and jury-duty evaders:

> Do not go stand in the assembly
> Do not stray to the very place of strife.
> It is precisely in strife that fate may overtake you;
> Besides, you may be made a witness for them.
> So that they take you along to testify in a lawsuit
> not your own. (Jacobsen, p. 25.)

Jacobsen believes that these democratic judicial institutions were not the vanguard of a vigorous democratic thrust but rather "a last stronghold, a stubborn survival, of ideas rooted in earlier ages." Thus, perhaps unwittingly, he refutes those who, while ostensibly advocating support of democracy for all nations, insist that it can only come with growth, progress, and development.

As Jacobsen looks backward in time at Mesopotamian history, "the competence and influence of the 'assembly' appears to grow and to extend from judiciary functions to other, even more vital, aspects of government." In the days of the kings of Akkad, "the assembly deemed it within its authority to choose a king." Farther back in older tradition concerning Uruk in the time of Gilgamesh, "beyond the border line of history proper," the ruler consults the assembly in important matters of peace and war. Gilgamesh, lord of Uruk, is remembered as consulting first the senate, "the elders of Uruk," and then the assembly, "the men of the town," before he decides to arm for a fight with King Agga of Kish. His consultation is not only for advice but for consent, and, Jacobsen correctly concludes, the assembly is recognized as "the ultimate political authority."(Jacobsen, p. 161.)

The success of the early Mesopotamian democratic thrust appears to be traceable to the fact that the egalitarian values of the primitive population were successfully translated into religious legend.

The Sumerians and the Akkadians projected their human terrestrial conditions into their world of gods and goddesses, who reflected early Mesopotamian culture by organizing themselves politically along democratic lines. There was, according to the Adad myth, an assembly of gods and goddesses usually held in a large court called *Ubshuukkinna*.

An, the god of heaven and "father of the gods," was their presiding officer, and Enlil, god of the storm, was their executive officer and discussion leader. There were fifty "senior gods"—corresponding to the earthly seniors of the Assyrian *karum*—who handled the discussion, and seven deciding "gods of fates," corresponding to the group of seven members of the *karum* entitled to seal documents.

The assembly's functions were not only judicial. It also had the authority to grant kingship and to take it back. The period of kingship was called a *bala*, the same word applied to the term of earthly Sumerian kings and—in its altered form *palu*—to that of the rulers of Akkad.

The elections of Mesopotamian kings of that period were dramatically confirmed as late as 1976 by the excavations which yielded the remains of the lost kingdom of Ebla, which flourished in 2500 B.C., a "large and thriving commercial, administrative, and intellectual center with economic and political institutions that sound remarkably familiar." (Chaim Bermant and Michael Weitzman, *Ebla: A Revelation in Archaeology*, excerpted in the *New York Times*, January 16, 1979, p. C–1.)

The diggings yielded some 15,000 clay tablets or fragments written in Sumerian cuneiform. The king of Ebla, according to the records discovered in the palace archives, was elected for a seven-year term and shared power with a council of elders. The king (we would probably call him President today) who lost reelection bids retired on a government pension!

What is involved here is not a primitive, prehierarchical society or a hierarchical society of limited scope—such as a village or even a town or city-state. Ebla, whose existence had long been inferred from Mesopotamian literature, now rises in history, through its own records, as a fairly extended kingdom of at least 250,000 inhabitants—a large population in those days—with a capital city of 30,000 residents "of whom eleven thousand seven hundred were civil servants." It was a society of highly organized sophistication. The findings included Sumerian-Eblaite dictionaries of more than 3,000 words, expense accounts of traveling diplomats, and even a list of beers, one of which was called *ebla*, "pronounced just like the city," write Bermant and Weitzman, venturing to add the obvious observation "could it have been the beer that made Ebla famous?" (Bermant and Weitzman, p. 159.)

Ebla appears to have hosted international conferences and dominated many other kingdoms and cities politically and economically. Among its principal trading partners were the cities of Sodom and Gomorrah, whose historical reality had been doubted until now.

So the thrust of Mesopotamian democracy, which even its enthusiastic commentator Jacobsen would cautiously trace as a declining tradition from "beyond the border line of history proper," now receives even stronger confirmation in recorded history than that which already had been found for it by Jacobsen and, after him, Oppenheim.

A little less than 4,000 years before the maturing of British Parliamentarism, the founding of the Swiss Confederation, and the birth of the American republic, we find in Mesopotamia a likeness of a political system which, although with much cruder and broader strokes of the brush, strikingly resembles the finer lines of the Swiss and American written constitutions and the unwritten charter of the British system.

On one fine but crucial point the Mesopotamian democracy may have been superior to at least the current Swiss system. The *Puhrum*, or assembly of the Babylonian gods, was open to goddesses. An old Babylonian hymn, the song of the goddess Ishtar, relates that "in their [i.e., the gods'] assembly her word is highly esteemed, is surpassing; she sits among them counting as much [with them] as Anum, their king." (Jacobsen, p. 163.) If the reality of the Babylonian system was, as we have seen above, but a reflection of the democratic legends of the Babylonian deities, then women may have participated in the earthly *Puhrum*. In Switzerland, women received the right to vote in the constitution only in 1971, and up to this writing they may not vote or even participate in some cantons in those open-air, popular assemblies for which Switzerland has had such a rightful claim to fame.

The Eblan discovery, as well as the Oppenheim and Jacobsen theses, may now enable us to cross the line between substance and form. As we move from the cradle of civilization to its neighbor, India, we may perhaps begin to feel entitled to suspect that, whether in form or substance, democracy may have been, indeed, the natural state of early man wherever he may have been.

4 India: The Spirit of Licchavis

At a cocktail party at the Egyptian Embassy in New Delhi, I met an Indian educator who told me, "I once headed a school in the state of Bihar only a few miles from the site of the first Indian democratic republic—that of the Licchavis, which existed 600 years B.C."

I had gone to India in January, 1984, to complete my research on early Indian democratic traditions on the village level. Arrangements had been made for me to visit the fabled Panchayat village organizations, descended directly from pre-British village India and now operating within the framework of modern Indian parliamentary democracy. I had not counted on being reminded that Indian democracy was already a reality of supravillage dimensions during the lifetime of the Buddha twenty-six centuries ago.

Licchavis was one of several such republics. Ten of them are mentioned by historians, who point to Pali and Jaina records as their sources:

1. The Sakyas of Kapilavatthu, settled on the border of Nepal and identified as the present Tilaura-kot.
2. The Bhaggas of Sumsumagiri, whose seat of power was in the district of Mirzapur.
3. The Bullis of Allakappa, located near the kingdom of Vethadipa, presumably between modern Shahabad and Muzzafarpur.

4. The Kalamas of Kesaputta, location unknown.
5. The Koliyas of Ramagama, to the east of Sakyas; the Koliyas and Sakyas once fought over the waters of the Rohini.
6. The Mallas of Pava, in the Gorakhpur District.
7. The Mallas of Kusinara, corresponding to the modern Kasia.
8. The Moriyas of Pipphalivana, said to have been a branch of the Sakyas.
9. The Videhas of Mithila, the present Janakapur, just within the Nepalese border.
10. The Licchavis of Vaisali, or modern Masarh, in the Muzzafarpur District in the State of Bihar.

(See Ramashankar Tripathi, *History of Ancient India*. Delhi: Motilal Banarsidass, 1942.)

By the second century, the Licchavis had extended their rule to Nepal with kings who "were masters but also servants of the people" and could be deposed by the people if they "could not prove themselves worthy of the trust placed in them." (Laldhos Deosa Rai, "Human Rights Development in Ancient Nepal," *Human Rights Quarterly*, vol. 3, no. 3, Summer, 1981, pp. 40–41.)

Siddhartha Gautama, later known as the Buddha, the enlightened one, was the son of Siddhohana, the *raja* of the Sakyas, and thus was commonly regarded as a prince. However, noted conservative Indian intellectual and political figure Minoo Masani, with whom I renewed an old friendship in Bombay, reminds us that although "we are often taught that Buddha's father was a king, that is not so." Masani asserts,

He was really the elected president of a republic. The misunderstanding is due to the fact that he was called a *raja*, which today means king. In those days, *raja* meant only ruler and was a term used to describe presidents of republics as well as kings. (Minoo Masani, *Our Growing Human Family*. Calcutta: Oxford University Press, 1981, p. 66.)

Since the Buddha sprang from the Sakyas, Buddhist writings provide more details of this stock. A summary from the writings of the political system of the Sakyas by historian Tripathi reads like excerpts from the U.S. Constitution and *Robert's Rules of Order*:

> The business of the clan was carried on in the open assemblies in *Santhagaras* or *Mote-halls*, where the young and the old, the rich and the poor alike were present. The Buddhist works give us a vivid idea of how deliberations were conducted in these assemblies, which were modeled on the religious *Samghas*. We learn that there were regular meetings with proper seating arrangements made by a special officer called *asanapannapaka* or *asanaprajnapaka*. Each meeting to be valid must have the requisite number of members present, but the chairman (*Vinayadhara*) was not counted for the purpose of the quorum. It was the duty of the whip (*Ganapuraka*) to complete the quorum by requisitioning the presence of members.
>
> The business began with the formal presentation (*sthanapanam*) of the motion (*natti or jnapti*), which was followed by a proclamation (*anussavanam*). Discussion related to the motion only, and all cantankerous and irrelevant talk was avoided and checked. A resolution (*pratijna*) received one reading (*jnapti-dvitiya-kamma*) and sometimes even three (*jnapti-catuttha-kamma*). Silence of the members on the resolution was regarded as assent, but in case of disagreement they had recourse to various devices, like referring the matter to a committee, with a view to arriving at a unanimous decision.
>
> If no unanimity was possible, votes (*chanda*) were taken. Voting was by tickets (*salaka*), generally slips of wood, of various colours to indicate different views.... Voting was perfectly free and unfettered, and the majority view (*ye-bhuyya-sikam*) prevailed. A question once decided was not to be reopened.... The procedure was thus democratic, anticipating in many respects the working of modern popular assemblies. (Tripathi, pp. 87–88.)

The title *raja* appears to have been broadly applied not only to kings and presidents alike but also to members of governing bodies with presumably legislative as well as executive functions. The Licchavis were known to have a governing body comprising 7,707 *rajas* and "were noted for their full and frequent assemblies, and they carried discussions in a spirit of confidence and concord." (Tripathi, p. 86.)

The resolute democratic character of these republics was reflected in the indigenous common term by which they were known—*gana-rajya*. *Rajya* meant the state or kingdom, *gana* meant numbers, and the combined term conveyed the concept "of a state where numbers or the masses of the people ruled—that is, a democracy." (Masani, p. 66.) The assertive republican democracy of the time of Buddha, however, was preceded in Indian history by institutions that flourished as early as the Vedic Age, two to three thousand years B.C., and which were the framework for the surviving thrust of the egalitarian traditions of the early society in confrontation with the autocratic drive of the hierarchical society.

Passages from the *Rigveda*, the earliest literary production of the Aryans, the race that settled and dominated India in those millennia, speak of rulers who appear to have been powerful indeed, called *samrat*, or emperor, as well as *visvasya bhuvanasya raja*, or ruler of the whole world. He lived in a grand palace and exacted heavy fines and punishment for petty crimes. His despotic network included envoys (*dutas*) and spies (*spas*).

Yet the *Rigveda* also gives great prominence to the popular assemblies called *samiti*, which included the common people, and the *sabha*, which appears to have been a more select body composed of the aristocracy—striking predecessors of the British Commons and House of Lords. Masani prefers to call the *sabha* (which he translates as "a body of men shining together") an elected parliament. (The *sabha* is now part of the name for the Indian parliament in New Delhi—the *Lok Sabha*.) An Indian historian states,

> The larger number of passages [of the *Rigveda*] which refer to them leave no doubt that they wielded great power and authority in administration, and worked as great checks to the exercise of arbitrary power by the king. Political affairs were freely discussed in these bodies and debates ran high, everyone wishing to convert others to his faith. (R. C. Majumdar, *Ancient India*. Delhi: Motilal Banarsidass, 1982, p. 25.)

Occasionally, the king was elected by the *vis*, the districts made up of kingship villages called *grama*. The democratic practices and popular assemblies, however, went into decline as the Aryan tribes consolidated their kingdoms and fortified their administrative systems. An historian writes,

The old tribal assemblies are still from time to time referred to, but their power was waning rapidly, and by the end of [the later Vedic] period, the king's autocracy was in most cases only limited by the power of the brahmans [the aristocratic caste], the weight of tradition, and the force of public opinion, which was always of some influence in ancient India. [Nevertheless] *ganas*, or tribal republics, survived for many centuries in outlying districts. (A.L. Basham, *The Wonder That Was India*. Delhi: Fontana Books, 1982, p. 42.)

In the days of the Epic Kings, the *sabha* was reduced to providing consultation on military matters. However, the *Mahabharata*, one of the two great epics of the age (along with the *Ramayana*), refers to the *gana* ("rule of the many") form of government as an apparent flourishing reality of the times. (*Santiparvan*, 107: 6–32.) They managed to prosper by "respecting established custom and usages"—a stubborn survival of the original cake of custom in a subcontinent dominated by autocrats. Sometimes the *ganas* even formed confederations (*samgha*). Chapter 81 of the *Santiparvan* represents Krisna as head of a *Gana* league, the *Andhaka-Vrisni*. (Tripathi, p. 71.)

By the end of the fifth century B.C., republics had disappeared from the subcontinent. Strong, centralized monarchies prevailed in the Mauryan Period (c. 324 B.C.–A.D. 320) during which ideas of kingship underwent significant changes.

At the beginning of the period a king was regarded as a mere mortal, though a mortal favored by the deities. Asoka, the great Mauryan emperor, styled himself and his forebears as *devanampiya*, beloved of the gods. Ironically, it was the Greeks, striking out from their democratic Hellenic bases, who may have first prodded Indian royalty to cross the tenuous line between divine favor to divinity itself.

Alexander, king of Macedon, initiated this process when, after his first great victory on Indian soil in 326 B.C., he spared the life of his gallant adversary, the king of Paurava, and generously gave him back his kingdom. Thenceforth, the Greeks would seek to use, rather than destroy, Indian royalty in their conquering march. This technique of strengthening conquered local despots in order to govern through them, this preference for "dealing with one man as long as he is our man" would later find emulation by the Romans in Jerusalem and much later by the British in India itself, as well as by other Western Europeans and by Americans in Africa, Latin America, and Asia. It was predictable irony, then, that the Greeks should introduce Indian emperors to titles like "divine king" and "god-like queen." (Majumdar, Raychaudhuri, and Datta, *An Advanced History of India*. Delhi: Macmillan, 1978, p. 117.)

However, the awesome combination of Greek imperialism and native autocracy could not stamp out altogether the uninterrupted development of democratic traditions in the local Indian communities. Indian monarchs, like their imperial counterparts in neighboring China, were the very model for the historian's perception of the central despot, satisfied with taxes and concubines, willingly permitting autonomy in villages which they, in any case, could not govern on a daily basis because of primitive communications and difficult terrain.

Among the most quoted sources for Indian history are the recorded narratives of Chinese Pilgrims who visited India to worship at hallowed Buddhist sites. One of these, Yuan Chwang, roamed India from A.D. 629 to A.D. 645. He called on the king of Harsa, whose huge realm covered the present Indian states of eastern Punjab, Uttar Pradesh, Bihar, Bengal, and Orissa. The king maintained an elaborate bureaucracy to exercise control over his vast empire including viceroys (*rajasthaniya*), governors (*lokapala*), and feudatories (*samanta*) for outlying provinces. "A commission of officers held the land," wrote the Chinese Pilgrim. Yet, Yuan Chwang also observed that the people were "left free to grow in their own surroundings unfettered by the shackles of overgovernment." He saw taxation as "light" with the main source of revenue being the traditional one-sixth of the produce and "duties at ferries and barrier stations." (Will Durant, *Our Oriental Heritage*. New York: Simon and Schuster, 1954, p. 421.)

Unshackling the people from overgovernment could hardly have been the objective of the king's intricate central government network, and it is safe to conclude that the local autonomy which Yuan Chwang admired was less the effect of a benign imperial policy than a concession imposed on the central government by the geographic realities of the territory.

So Indian republics and Indian kingdoms came and went and so did the Greeks, the Moghuls, and British, depositing in urban India their often transitory contributions to the politics and the culture of the people. Through all these transitions, however, one thing stubbornly remained—the reality of village India where for unbroken millennia the people lived by democratic consensus and customary law.

5 The Stubborn Village

"Just because a man is poor and maybe cannot read does not mean he does not care for his human rights," an Indian villager told the *New York Times* shortly before the elections that were to end the two-year emergency declared by Indira Gandhi. The Congress government had "tried to shut my mouth this last year and a half," and therefore he was going to vote for the opposition. The opposition won.

The conventional image of India is that of one vast, impoverished, overpopulated land where the poor are concerned only with filling their half-empty stomachs and couldn't care less for the right to vote or free speech. This "full-belly" theory has been disproved over and over again by massive turnouts of poor voters in developing countries all over the world. In rebuttal, proponents of the theory would explain away the turnouts as leftover reflexes of habits implanted by the former colonial master.

The rebuttal cannot hold for areas like Central America, where the Spaniards left no electoral tradition, nor can it hold for the village voter in India where British rule did not encourage rural participation in the parliamentary process and was successful in local government only in so far as it built on the traditional village structures of consensual democracy. The tradition of free choice that the poor Indian voter in the *New York Times* story was seeking to recapture was not a British but an indigenous Indian value, one more ancient and more durable than village traditions in Britain itself.

The *trinoda necessitas* in Anglo-Saxon life developed self-governing villages, but they were the work essentially of invaders, and the indigenous feudal system made short work of them. The bedrock of the village democracy was the commonly owned land, but feudal policy of land "enclosures" extinguished the rights of future generations in commonly held arable land and the village greens.

Even in Germany, where autonomy was enjoyed by entire cities which formed the famous voluntary leagues, no effective resistance could finally be offered to the dominant absolutism. In France, the power of the crown was such that only local bodies chartered by the king could flourish. Public law provided that communal taxes could be levied only with the consent of the king. By contrast, in India the right of the local community to levy communal taxes was always respected by all central governments before British rule.

The Indian village assembly, an institution that was developed as early as during the ancient Munda-Dravidian culture, persisted until the late eighteenth century when British rule attempted its own modified system of local government. As in China and Russia, writes an Indian sociologist, even under

> strong and influential kingdoms... village assemblies were left to enjoy their autonomy as long as they collected the revenue or tax (which they themselves apportioned among the inhabitants) and sent it to the royal treasury. The supreme government dealt with the village assemblies, not with the inhabitants. (Radhakamal Mukerjee, *Democracies of the East*. New Delhi, 1923, p. 197.)

Historians have found scant records of the composition of North Indian village councils, but there is ample evidence of the character and structure of their southern counterparts, which varied according to local custom. In the Cola kingdom at Uttaramerur, the village was divided into thirty wards or sections, each choosing its representative to the council by lot, or sortition, an electoral device practiced in early Greek democracies. (Some authors such as Majumdar claim bigger council memberships in some specific instances—300, 312, and as many as 1,000.)

The council was then divided into five committees, "the first three of which were responsible for gardens and orchards, tanks and irrigation, and the settlement of disputes respectively, while the functions of the last two are uncertain." (A.L. Basham, *The Wonder That Was India*. Delhi: Fontana Books, 1982, p. 107.)

Majumdar lists recorded titles of "more important committees":

1. Great men elected for the year.
2. Great men elected for charities.
3. Great men elected for tanks.
4. Great men elected for gardens.
5. Great men elected for supervision of justice.
6. Great men elected for gold supervision.
7. Great men elected for supervision of wards.
8. Great men elected for supervision of fields.
9. Great men elected for management of temples.
10. Great men elected for supervision of ascetics.

(R.C. Majumdar, *Ancient India*. Delhi: Motilal Banarsidas, 1982, p. 125.)

The first committee was also called "Annual Supervision Committee" and probably managed general affairs not covered by the other committees. The council members received no pay and were subject to recall for misconduct. As in some modern Western societies, including nineteenth- and twentieth-century United States, there was a property qualification for office—a house and a small plot of land. The age limits were thirty-five and seventy and membership was all male. However, Majumdar refers to a recorded instance of a woman member of the Committee of Justice.

The constitutions of Uttaramerur villages provided for safeguards against corruption and monopoly of power. After a year of service a council member could not be returned to office until after three years. In one case, the retiree's relatives were disqualified from election for five years, in another for ten.

According to a ninth-century inscription, some chiefs at war entered into an agreement with a village headman to look to the peace of the villages under their protection and to pay a fine of one hundred *panam* if any villager was injured. The monarch was forced to respect village laws, interfering only in cases of gross mismanagement or embezzlement of communal funds.

In South India three classes of local assemblies appear to have existed: the *urar*, or general village assembly; the *nagarattar* of the merchants and professionals; and the *nattar*, or district assembly, which acted on problems of interest to the whole district. The assemblies would meet in the *sabha-mandapams* of the temples or under the *pipal* or olive tree.

The original Munda-Dravidian village system was assimilated by the political institutions of the Aryan village community, producing the lasting, compact, and efficient foundations of Indo-Aryan polity. The village assemblies survived all changes in the central government—through the Mauryan imperial bureaucracy, the Moghul despots, the Muslim theocrats, to British rule.

The Muslim Sultan in India

in practice was a perfect autocrat, unchecked by any restrictions; and his word was law. [But] his direct influence was limited to the areas within striking distance of his forts and outposts, and the distant provinces were placed in the charge of viceroys, who were called Naib Sultans. (R.C. Majumdar, H.C. Raychaudhuri, and Kalikinkar Datta, *An Advanced History of India*. Delhi: Macmillan, 1978, p. 384.)

Even the Naib Sultans could not exercise total control over their territories.

Large tracts of land had of necessity to be left in the hands of old Hindu chieftains who were not interfered with in ruling their ancestral territories so long as they sent tributes and presents to Delhi. The village communities continued unaffected by the establishment of a new government in the country. (Majumdar, Raychaudhuri, and Datta, p. 388.)

The British introduced the *Ryotwari*, a sort of permanent settlement system intended to revamp the revenue collection network, but it only partially eclipsed and could not supplant the ancient village system. By the 1920s, indigenous village assemblies were still seen administering public property, i.e., temples, village endowments, and forming courts of justice for small civil suits and petty criminal offenses.

Local government terms coming down from pre-British Indo-Aryan-Dravidian polity still persisted, such as *sabha* or *samiuham* for village assembly, *maha-mukham orkula* for caste assembly, *vadi* for plaintiff, *pratibadi* for accused, *pari, desha dhe pati, senapati, pradhani, buddhimanta, kula-ejman* for headman of caste or village, *grama-panam, grama-samudayam* for village funds, and *adhikari* for secretary. In the south, each of the thirty members of the *sabha* or village assembly was still voted upon by ten families, and there was still an executive committee of nine, the *nirvaha sabha*, presided over by a *gramani*.

Neither sultan nor *raja*, nor moghul nor British *raj*, ever proved equal to the stubborn democracy of the ancient Indian village.

6 The *Panchayat*: Gandhi vs. Britain

The most durable vehicle for independent democratic consensus in the Indian village has been the *panchayat*, the institution in India I visited in January, 1984. *Panchayat* means a "body of five good men, elected by the people, and having both executive and judicial functions." (Indira Rothermund, *The Aundh Experiment.* Delhi: Somiaya Publications, 1983, p. 56.) The modern version gives it additional developmental functions.

The *Panchayat* was aired and fostered by the now-fabled incapacity of the Buddhist and Hindu rulers to reach out and actually govern remote villages and offer them more than tax collection activities. The five good men (the actual number varied according to custom and size of village—*panch*, five, was the traditional sacred number in Indian culture) formulated codes of conduct for village affairs consistent with custom and equity. (Rothermund, p. 56.)

During the Moghul period, the *Panchayats*, under a village headman called *Mukadam*, exercised full authority in the settlement of disputes, besides discharging managerial affairs over education, public health, religious endowments, and such. (Rothermund, p. 56.) Researchers note the "rare and remarkable phenomenon of the state and village organizations coexisting... as distinct entities in the mainstream of national, popular, and collective life," with the state "insisting, of course, on regular payment of taxes." (Rothermund, p. 56.)

A society with such an orderly division of the task of government between state and village was not what Karl Marx perceived in India from London. Marx saw peasant societies as formed "by simple addition of homologous magnitudes, much as potatoes in a sack form a sackful of potatoes." (Lloyd and Susanne Rudolph, *The Modernity of Tradition*. Chicago: University of Chicago Press, 1967, p. 17.)

Marx thought of peasants as a vast mass, knowing each other only parochially and because of lack of "a natural union" incapable of political organization.

> They cannot represent themselves, they must be represented... [and] their representatives must at the same time appear as their master, as an authority over them, as an unlimited governmental power that protects them against other classes and sends the rain and the sunshine from above. (Rudolph and Rudolph, p. 18.)

So, in 1853, Marx saw Britain's mission in India as one of destruction and of regeneration—the annihilation of the old Asiatic society and the laying of the material foundations of Western society in Asia. However, for Marx that mission of annihilation was still incomplete. He wrote,

> We know that the municipal organization [village and caste *panchayats*, or councils] and the economical basis of the village communities have been broken up, but their worst feature, the dissolution of society into stereotype and disconnected atoms [that is, the Indian villages and castes], has survived... the revolutionary impact of British imperialism. (Rudolph and Rudolph, p. 23.)

Marx expected that, with the help of British colonialism, this feature too would disappear in India, paving the way for the Westernization and socialization of the society. He analyzed the problem of modernization in India using the exact parameters within which he had been viewing European society. He saw Europe progressing only when European traditional corporate structures were atomized and replaced by individualized classes and national communities whose "ills, exploitations, and alienations would in turn be repaired by communism's voluntary corporate structures." It is interesting to note that the Rudolphs suggest that "new historiography may want to investigate whether traditional Western corporatism was ever so effectively destroyed as this theory holds." (Rudolph and Rudolph, p. 23.)

Unaware as they probably were of the mission of annihilation assigned to them by Marx, the British did attempt, in any case, to carry it out. British rule put an end to the isolation and democratic autonomy of Indian villages. With improved communications, the market economy gradually replaced the village economy, and the British introduced their own institutions of local self-government designed to accommodate colonial policies. They resisted the revival of the village *panchayats*, arguing that, as the 1909 Decentralization Commission Report put it, "the reestablishment of village *panchayats* would serve as a vehicle for the emergence of an unorthodox system of village governments, not necessarily conducive to a wholesome growth of the British Empire." (Rothermund, p. 57.)

It was not till 1919 that some provinces were permitted to revive *panchayats*, in which adult males were entitled to vote. However, whenever there was an elected chairman, the central government took pains to appoint a special executive officer invested with the actual authority to administer the village. (Rothermund, p. 58.) "In short," Rothermund points out, "under the centralized British system of government in India, the local bodies could not enjoy autonomous powers, and the question of local autonomy remained a subject of controversy." (Rothermund, p. 58.)

Such revealing revisionism should temper somewhat the alacrity with which some Western observers, among them Kennan and Buckley, would dismiss current democratic aspirations in non-Western countries as rootless leftovers of transplanted Western values. What the British did in India, as we shall see later, was essentially duplicated by France, Spain, Holland, Germany, Portugal in Asia, Africa and Latin America. Democratic forms, developed in postfeudal Europe, were transplanted to the colonies, but at the same time indigenous democratic substance was drained of its life blood and often totally destroyed.

It took full Indian independence for the original village democracy to return to India. Mahatma Gandhi, as early as 1916, had wished that "the village *panchayats* would now be a living force in a special way and India would soon enjoy self-government suited to its requirements." (Rothermund, p. 35.) However, his struggle to introduce the village *panchayat* system into the Indian Constitution was not an easy one.

There were bitter opponents of decentralization, like Ambedkar, one of the "founding fathers," who sneered at the village as "a sink of localism, a den of ignorance, narrowmindedness and communalism," a strongly offensive view for which some Gandhi followers, with typical nonviolent restraint, charged Ambedkar with being "urban high-brow." (Rothermund, p. 36.)

In the end, Gandhi's drive triumphed and the *panchayat* was enshrined in the constitution as the basis for Indian democratic reconstruction. There seemed to be no other way to govern India, a nation so vast and so disparate in culture and tongue, and today, thirty years later, the choice appears to be vindicated.

Rejecting Marx's prescription of annihilation of traditional structures and building solidly on freedom and human rights, India, in spite of still so much visible poverty and continuing communal strife, which erupts in climactic violence such as the recent assassination of Indira Gandhi, is achieving industrial growth which outstrips that of China, whose development strategy accepted Marx's prescription and sacrificed human values but whose poverty is there, although not as visible as in Mother Teresa's candid community in Calcutta. (See Simon Leys, *Chinese Shadows*. New York: The Viking Press, 1977.)

This democratic village system, the *panchayati raj*, occupies a three-tiered structure fairly uniform in every State of India and with elective bodies named after ancient Indian deliberative assemblies. For example, the village *panchayat* is called the *gram-sabha*, elected by adult suffrage. The chairmen of all *gram-sabhas* located in one block (a group of about one hundred villages) make up the middle tier, the *panchayat samiti*. *Sabha* and *samiti* were names known in ancient times. The top tier, the *zilla parishad*, is the point of contact between the villages and the state and federal government. It is made up of all the *samiti* chairmen found in one district, members of the parliament, officials of education, and state legislators whose constituencies fall in the district.

In the historic city of Poona, in the State of Maharashtra, I was accompanied to a model *panchayat* by C. S. Natu, chairman of the *zilla parishad* of the district. It was located about five kilometers from the city, in a village called Dhayari, birthplace of the late Prime Minister Bahadur Shastri. My wife and I were received by the *panchayat* officials with traditional flower garlands and asked to sit on chairs while the members of the *panchayat* sat on the floor, as they would during their periodic deliberations. Very little English was understood by the gathering, and Mr. Natu had to undertake extensive interpreting from Maharati.

The villagers seemed proudly aware of the deep historical roots of their *panchayat*. There was mention of the *gaon sabha*, the ancient village assembly attended by all village adults. Some even remembered the *gana rajya*, the name applied to very early Indian city republics centuries before Christ. Mr. Natu remarked that British-style democracy in India had "halted at British level." Indeed, there was nothing to be seen in Dhayari of that very model of the modern Indian gentleman, sipping his late afternoon whiskey at his favorite Bombay club. This was the original India, and there was nothing alien or imported about it.

From Poona we proceeded to Bangalore where, after meeting with the Secretary for Rural Development of the State of Karnataka, officials drove us to the Chokkasandra *Panchayat*, two hours north of the city. We were now in South India, where more copious records have been kept of the activities of pre-British *panchayats*.

In Harohali, we visited a block level (*taluka*) *panchayat samiti*. The local language was Kannada, but perhaps because we were dealing with a block level organization, we sensed a higher understanding of English than at the village *panchayat* in Poona. The block embraced five villages with a population of 3,600. There were thirteen elected members of the *samiti*, with two seats reserved for women and, in accordance with the Indian Constitution, two for representatives of "scheduled" (economically backward) castes.

The new *samiti* chairman was a thirty-year-old man, B. Venkatarayapa, but his predecessor, Mr. Ardodapaya, who was present at the meeting, had retired at the age of eighty after having been in office through successive reelections for thirty-five years. Mr. Ardodapaya still remembered pre-independence days when the village headman was not elected but appointed by the British colonial government.

In this particular village where the meeting was being held, all except five Muslim families were Hindus. There seemed to be harmonious coexistence in the represented villages between Hindus, Muslims, and Christians (Christianity has a substantial following in South India). The voting and decision-making on the village and block levels appeared not to follow national party lines, further dramatizing the stubborn, indigenous strains of the village democracy.

This is not to understate the pervasive impact of the British ethos on Indian life. When the distinguished Indian Socialist leader S. M. Joshi spoke to me about "his queen" in Poona, and I innocently asked whom he meant, he replied in mock surprise at my ignorance: "The real queen, of course, the one who sits in London, not that empress [Indira Gandhi] in New Delhi!"

There is, of course, much of what Britain left that keeps Indians going. However, popular democracy must deal with the folk level, and that appears to have been for all those 200 years of occupation mostly below "British level." Furthermore, the Indian who managed to travel to Britain could not have missed those features of British society which were, in fact, striking duplications of the inequalities among the peoples of India. British class distinction (including, as Professor Higgins would lament, that multilevel "verbal class distinction" inside the confines of London itself) was hardly an inspiration to a solution to that apparent contradiction to village democracy— the Indian caste system.

7 Varna and *Pygmalion*

The abbreviation RP (Received Pronunciation) denotes the speech of educated people living in London and the southeast of England and of other people elsewhere who speak in this way. If the qualifier 'educated' be assumed, RP is then a regional (geographical) dialect, as contrasted with London Cockney, which is a class (social) dialect. (*Encyclopedia Britannica, Micropedia*, vol. 6, 1973, p. 883.)

The article hastens to add, as if to hedge against charges of superciliousness, that RP is not intrinsically superior to other varieties of English.

George Bernard Shaw's Professor Higgins definitely thought otherwise. Apparently contradicting his creator's social reformism, Shaw's Pygmalion spent sleepless nights proving he could transform a London Cockney girl into a proper English lady by teaching her how to stop dropping her hs and speak *RP* English. His class consciousness transcended the linguistic urban limits of London. He sniffed at the Scotch and the Irish who, as he sang in the musical comedy version, "leave you close to tears" with their spoken English, and at the Americans who "haven't used it for years."

British class distinction was so pervasive it accompanied English settlements in the New World where the colonists were supposed to start a new life in equality and freedom. A recent documentary by the Public Broadcasting System in the United

States showed the colonists in Jamestown, Virginia, finding a way of practicing class discrimination even under socially leveling conditions of pioneering life. While everyone in the settlement was forced to eat the same food because of scant provisions, the gentlemen ate under constructed shades with spoons and forks while the commoners had to eat with their hands in the broiling sun!

London, Marx's own social laboratory, failed to carry out his assignment for progress—the atomization of traditional class structures. As we have seen, Britain also failed that Marxian expectation in India. Whether in London or in India, the result was not "the prime law of stagnation" predicted by Marx, for the Rudolphs may now write of India that it "has shown a strong propensity to transform rather than supersede traditional corporate structures, to move imperceptibly from traditional to modern corporatism without so marked an intervening individualist phase as the West is said to have experienced." (Lloyd and Susanne Rudolph, *The Modernity of Tradition*. Chicago: University of Chicago Press, 1967, p. 123.) The same, however, could be written of India's assigned "atomizer," Britain, whose social classes, through the slow, evolutionary development of the parliamentary process, have become effective protagonists in the work of national construction.

In fact, the ancient historical roots of British and Indian social divisions would be discovered to have been overlapping. About 2000 B.C., the great steppes from Poland to Central Asia were inhabited by tall, fair-skinned, semi-nomadic barbarians who called themselves Aryas, now anglicized into Aryans. Unlike the civilizations of Sumer and the city-states of Harappa and Mohenjo Daro along the Indus River, whose mobility was limited by their reliance on lumbering four-wheeled carts drawn by asses, the Aryans had learned to tame the horse and harnessed it to a light chariot. With this speedy vehicle, frightening to those who would first encounter it, they migrated in all directions, westward to the British Isles (giving Ireland its original name of Eire, a variation of Arya), and southward to India, spawning new nations—Greeks, Latins, Celts, Teutons, and Indians.

When the Aryans entered India (as when their descendant

Celts crossed the channel to the British Isles), they brought with them a class division which was already a reality in their tribal structure. The earliest Aryan hymns handed down by tradition in India sing of the *ksatra*, the nobility, and the *vis*, the ordinary tribesmen. (A.L. Basham, *The Wonder That Was India*. Delhi: Fontana Books, 1982, p. 35.) Records of other Indo-European peoples suggest that Indo-European premigratory society already featured a tribal aristocracy.

In India, fair-skinned Aryanism had an early encounter with peoples of darker color, including the Dasas and Dasyus, survivors of the Harappa culture. In what may have been the first precedent for Hitler's assertion of master race status for the Aryan race, the first Indian Aryans appeared to have stressed racial purity when confronted with the darker Dasas. Class divisions were hardened. Those Aryans who intermarried with the Dasas also lost some social standing. At the same time the priests among the pure Aryans began to arrogate more privileges as the complex sacrificial lore began to require greater skill and training.

By the end of the Rigvedic Period (about 600 B.C.), Indian society was divided into four great classes: priest (*brahmana*), warrior (*ksatriya*), peasant (*vaisya*), and serf (*sudra*). The classes survive to the present day, and the Sanskrit term for them is *varna*, which means color, suggesting their origin in shades of skin complexion.

However, *varna* classes are not castes. The term *caste* in fact was first applied to Indian community groups by the Portuguese, who in the sixteenth century began to call them *castas*, meaning tribes, clans, or families. What the Portuguese perceived was not the social division originally springing from skin complexions but a complex and proliferating web of social groupings identified indigenously as *jati* and governed in their relations by three rules of varying rigidity: endogamy, or legitimate marriage only within the group; commensality, receiving food from and eating it in the presence of members of the same or higher group; and craft-exclusiveness, each person living by his own group's trade or profession and not by that of any other. The last rule appears to be the best available guide to tracing the castes' origins.

Historians appear to have first traced castes to the meticulous cataloguing of trades and professions in late Vedic literature, "as if their members were looked on almost as distinct species." (Basham, p. 150.) Tribal associations, new racial infusions into the society, and the development of new crafts combined with the occupational group consciousness to create for India an almost impossible, complex social structure. Some authors, such as Prof. J. H. Hutton, attempt to simplify understanding of the castes, viewing the system "as an adaptation of one of the most primitive of social relationships, whereby a small clan, living in a comparatively isolated village, would hold itself aloof from its neighbors by a complex series of taboos." Hutton has found "embryonic caste features in the social structure of some of the hill tribes of present-day India." (Basham, p. 151.) However, the caste system is not a peculiarly Hindu phenomenon. Followers of other religions known for their egalitarian tenets, Muslims, Sikhs, and Kerala Christians, have not succeeded in eluding caste.

The last fifty years have seen real signs of the beginnings of a dismantling of the old Hindu social order, but it is not a revolutionary dismantling. India appears to be undergoing a period during which the caste system has managed to transform itself into an instrument for democratization.

"Caste," write the Rudolphs, "that most pervasive and, for most students of Indian society, Marxian and non-Marxian alike, most retrograde of India's social institutions has not only survived the impact of British imperialism but also transformed and transvalued itself." Indeed, in some ways castes have been "inimical to the realization of political democracy" in India. However, the Rudolphs point out, there is "extensive and weighty evidence [that they] have contributed more to its realization than its inhibition." (Rudolph and Rudolph, p. 126.) The Rudolphs ascribe to the caste a strong role in each of three types of political mobilization in Indian democratic society: vertical, horizontal, and differential.

Vertical mobilization is described as "the marshaling of political support by traditional notables in local societies that are organized and integrated by rank, mutual dependence, and the legitimacy of traditional authority." The role of the caste in this level of mobilization is compared to that of the traditional elites in Britain, the "characteristically territorial aristocracy and gentry, [who] turned traditional loyalty and economic dependence to good account by mobilizing dependents and inferiors." The Indian traditional elites are said to have "responded to representative government and popular politics by mobilizing what local notables in Britain called their 'interest.'" (Rudolph and Rudolph, p. 25.)

In carrying out horizontal mobilization, the "marshaling of popular political support by class or community leaders and their specialized organizations," the caste system has developed a transformed version of its component castes—the caste association. The Rudolphs characterize these caste associations as "paracommunities" which enable members "to pursue social mobility, political power, and economic advantage." (Rudolph and Rudolph, p. 27.)

In this form the caste has ceased to be a purely ascriptive group where birth is sufficient condition for membership. The *jati* now takes on the features of a voluntary association similar to Western counterparts, which include an overt act of "joining," as opposed to just being "born into." Joining includes financial support for the association's activities, attending meetings, and voting for candidates supported by the association leadership.

These caste associations, finally, facilitate "differential mobilization" of political support by political parties. They provide the parties with organized campaign areas and in many cases ensure that the parties choose candidates from their organized ranks.

Caste then becomes a propellant, rather than a deterrence, to the advance of democratic politics. In this way, they parallel the historic role of social classes in the development of European representative democracy.

It was the dynamic interaction between monarchy, nobility, and commoner that produced the beginnings of representative democracy in Europe in the twelfth century. At least one author believes that it did not begin in England but that "the assemblies of Spain pointed the way." (Bertie Wilkinson, ed., *The Creation of Medieval Parliaments*. New York: John Wiley and Sons, 1900, p. 5.) Commoners' representatives were first summoned to the Cortes, Spain's fledgling parliament, by King Alfonso IX in 1188. His motive in inviting them was not altogether a democratic altruism. He wanted to pit them against the power of the nobility.

Wilkinson notes that while this had the effect of rendering the Cortes a more democratic character, it served to weaken the nobility, "one of the more important restraints on the power of the ruler and thus strengthened the tendency towards absolute rule." (Wilkinson, p. 7.) Thus, the perennial rivalry between monarchy and nobility served as a catalyst for the emergence of commoners as a political power and for their eventual recognition, however reluctant, by both monarchy and nobility as "equals" at least in the political if not in the social context. Eventually, the continuing interaction produced the permanent institutionalization of representative democracy.

Until the Marxist states of the world are able to achieve the elusive goal of a classless society, which was the vision of their prophet, instead of stagnating in a dictatorship of the proletariat and creating—in the words of one of its disillusioned disciples, Milovan Djilas—a New Class, social classes are a reality which humankind will have to live with for some time.

Whether in England, India, or the United States, the struggle to close the gap between the classes is being made possible by incorporating them in the "body politic" and permitting an evolutionary social amalgamation in the only system which makes that possible. That system was once wisely characterized by Winston Churchill as the worst form of government, except for all the others: democracy.

8 Confucius Said...?

In 1978, "democracy posters" made their appearance on Peking walls. They complained that Chinese "cannot tolerate human rights and democracy being only slogans belonging to the Western bourgeoisie while the Eastern proletariat supposedly needs nothing but dictatorship." (*The Washington Post*, November 23, 1978, p. 5.) The next year Chinese peasants demonstrated in Peking crying, "We want democracy and human rights!" (The *New York Times*, January 15, 1979, p. 11.)

Across the Taiwan straits, the indigenous Taiwanese whose ancestors had left China a millennium ago but who had preserved authentic Confucian traditions, had been demonstrating and struggling for years against the Taipei regime, seeking the institution of a democratic state independent of the mainland.

This democratic lunge against left and right has puzzled some Western observers who do not see any historical or cultural explanation for it. This urge for democracy must come from some acquired taste, it is argued, perhaps learned at the feet of Western Christian missionaries. It certainly could not be inspired by some native value, for it goes against the very grain of the Confucian history of China.

Even the respected Sinologist John K. Fairbank has claimed to observe a Chinese apathy toward democratic electoral processes. Noting that the Chinese have enough democracy through their civil service examination, he has written that "the Chinese don't believe in the kind of national horse race we call an election." (*China*, advertising supplement, The *Washington Post*, 1980).

A closer look at that history may tell a different story. In Chapter 1 we saw China as the consummate historical specimen of a state with an ostensibly powerful central government forced, by primitive communications, to permit local communities to govern themselves from day to day by their own customary law. Chinese village government was not much different from that of other cultures of Asia. At the top was a council of family heads. Village executive officials were elected or appointed.

Let us examine at random the terminology in one of myriads of locations and dialects, the four official leaders in the village in Taitou, Shantung Province: the *she-chang*, the *shwang-chang*, the *hsiang-yueh*, and the *ti-fang*. (See Martin C. Yang, *A Chinese Village*. London: Kegan Paul, Trench & Trubner & Co., 1948.)

The first two officials were elected by the villagers. The *she-chang* was head of the rural district who traveled with other village officers from one village to another and from his district to the county government to perform his duties. The *shwang-chang* was the head of the village. He had to be a native of the village in which he held office and was elected for a term of one year with unlimited reelection.

The *hsiang-yueh* was the tax collector, was appointed by the county government, and was not necessarily an inhabitant of the village. The *ti-fang* was the village policeman, appointed by the village elders and in charge of reporting criminal cases to the government, settling petty disputes, and "organizing night-patrol systems." For patent reasons, these two appointive officials, Yang reports, were not expected to enjoy a popular following among the villagers. As for the elective positions, some apathy, comparable to contemporary Western situations (i.e., barely more than 50 percent of registered voters casting their ballots in the 1980 U.S. presidential election), was to be noted. Applications for candidacies to elective positions were sometimes "so few that all those that were handed in had a good chance of success." (Yang, p. 10.)

"The people," writes Durant, "preferred to be ruled by custom, and to settle their disputes by face-saving compromises out of court." (Will Durant, *The Story of Civilization, Part I: Our Oriental Heritage.* New York: Simon and Schuster, 1954, p. 797.)

The autonomy of these local communities was extensive, as "whole villages and territories were left freedom to sign their own commercial charters and defensive agreements, to carry on education, sanitation, and public works in their natural social groupings." (Radhakamal Mukerjee, *Democracies of the East.* New Delhi, 1923, p. 181.)

However, if the similarity is striking between the Chinese village government in its democratic character and other Asian local communities, there is the point that is tenaciously made by serious social scientists that, granting the lack of central government control, substantial democracy could not have possibly flourished in local Chinese communities because of the pervasive, authoritarian drive of the Confucian ethic. The view from the West of this fascinating ethic is that its essence is harmony, induced by a strong sense of obligation at the top and of duty below. In microcosm, this harmony is perceptible in the family, within which absolute fidelity and obedience to the head is enjoined among all members.

Sweeping conclusions have been made from this unparticularized summary of Confucianism. For example, American columnist Joseph Kraft writes that the Confucian mode expects "either total acceptance or total rejection of authority." There is, he says, "no halfway house"; no such concept, as in the West, of a "loyal opposition." (Joseph Kraft, "The Confucian Connection," The *Washington Post*, June 20, 1983, op-ed page.)

With less basis in fact than in romance, Kraft credits the Confucian ethic with leaping overseas to Southeast Asia, thus rationalizing the "authoritarianism" in, for example, the Philippines. Filipinos will find all this amusing, remembering that, for unique historical reasons, Chinese culture, far from being embraced as relevant in their country is rejected and sometimes, unfortunately, despised. In any case, the diaspora of "Austronesians" in Southeast Asia took place before Confucius was born, and most of the contact between Chinese and Southeast Asians historically has been on the commercial level.

The absolute equation that somewhat impetuously has been drawn between Confucianism and conformism would appear to be founded on a fairly perfunctory perception of K'ung-fu-tze's philosophy of government. K'ung the Master, as his pupils called him, preached harmony and looked to the "natural social order provided by the family" as irreplaceable by any amount of state legislation. However, K'ung never taught absolute, unconditional, irrational obedience within the family. He taught, indeed, that society rests upon obedience of the children to their parents, and of the wife to her husband, and that "when that goes, chaos comes." (James Legge, *The Life and Teachings of Confucius*. London, 1985, p. 27.) For him, however, there was one thing higher than this law of obedience and that was the moral law.

So he counseled gradual but, if necessary, increasing opposition to unreasonable parental discipline. "In serving his parents," he suggested initially, "[a son] may remonstrate with them, but gently," but then, he allowed, "when [the son] sees that they [the parents] do not follow [his advice], he shows an increased degree of reverence, but does not abandon [his purpose]." Then, the ultimate precept: "When the command is wrong a son should resist his father," and when it is the emperor who is in error, "a minister should resist his August Master." (Brian Brown, *The Story of Confucius*, Philadelphia, 1927, p. 12.)

This is far from the "no halfway house, no loyal opposition" Confucianism beheld in Western eyes. Like the myth of the despotic club-swinging caveman, the fable of the stern, uncontestable father of the Chinese family, the reflection and cultural justification at the bottom of the equally uncontestable emperor at the top, has been accepted without question, inventively embellished, and utilized to validate modern repression.

What else is resisting a father without striking at him, resisting the emperor without slaying him but going into "loyal opposition?" Other family members may join in that opposition to the family head, as Pearl Buck, the American author who lived for decades in China, attests to from personal experience: "I have seen in a Chinese home a father, angered enough to strike a child, held back by other members, in the conviction that no child should be struck by an adult, since anger is an aberration and an angry act by an adult is a disgrace." (Pearl S. Buck, "Elements of Democracy in the Chinese Traditional Culture," *St. John's Papers*, New York: St. John's University, p. 3.)

When loyal opposition proves to be insufficient to bring about change at the top, then revolution becomes a divine right. This was the conclusion of the Confucian disciple Mencius, who remembered his Master had said that "if the people have no faith in their rulers, there is no standing for the state." (Durant, p. 672.)

The Master had explained his thesis on popular government while traveling to Wei with his disciple Tzu Kung:

Tzu Kung asked about government. Confucius said, "The essentials are sufficient food, sufficient troops, and the confidence of the people." Tzu Kung said, "Suppose you were forced to give up one of these three, which would you let go first?" Confucius said, "The troops." Tzu Kung asked again, "If you were forced to give up one of the two remaining, which would you let go?" Confucius said, "Food. For from old, death has been the lot of all men, but a people without faith cannot survive." (Sister Maria Ignazia Bunuan, ed., *We Chinese*. Taipei: St. Paul Publications, 1982, p. 25.)

In other words, the Chinese people were the actual and proper source of political sovereignty. This tenet was held 2,000 years before the Jeffersonian declaration which proclaimed the right of revolution against a "foreign" king, a position not quite as radical as advocacy of the right to slay one's own erring monarch.

Three centuries after K'ung's death, China began to experiment with its concrete expression of the Master's teaching on popular sovereignty—the civil service examinations opened to "all males of any age." Centuries later the British would imitate this democratizing device. In Britain it would not succeed in leveling classes. In China "the plan provided a perfect reconciliation between aristocracy and democracy; all men were to have an equal opportunity to make themselves fit for office, but office was to be open only to those who made themselves fit." (Durant, p. 799.)

An aristocratic class did exist in China, but, unlike its counterpart in England, its membership was neither fixed nor permanent. "Individuals were raised to the aristocratic class from the plebeian, and sank to plebeian status although they had been aristocrats," writes a University of Chicago historian. (Herrlee Glessner Creel, *The Birth of China*. New York: John Day, 1937, p. 25.)

> Kuan Tzu, the [Chou Dynasty] statesman... urged that all of the exceptionally able among the common people should be selected by the officials who supervised them, and raised into the *shih* class. On the other hand, wholesale reduction of families to the enslaved class, because of a crime of one of their members, was a penalty which always hung over the heads of the aristocrats. (Creel, p. 26.)

Thus, class distinction was ephemeral. Creel observes,

> The Discourses of the States quotes the son and heir of King Ling who, after reflecting that the sons and grandsons of many who formerly occupied high places were now tilling the soil while others who started as peasants were now in the government, concluded that "really, there is no difference between people of various classes." (Creel, p. 26.)

Certainly, the examinations for individuals stressed the importance of the individual, contradicting another interpretation of Confucian, and all Asian, society as group, rather person, oriented. "The Chinese people were certainly the most individualistic," states Pearl Buck, "and yet the most mutually considerate of all peoples."(Buck, p. 3.)

The ideal Confucian vision of China may have inspired the civil service examinations, but it went deeper than that. Civil servants are, of course, important—they run the bureaucracy—but what about political vision and leadership? What did the Master hold as the ideal Chinese society?

When the Great Principle [of the Great Similarity] prevails, the whole world becomes a republic; they elect men of talents, virtue, and ability; they talk about sincere agreement, and cultivate universal peace. Thus men do not regard as their parents only their own parents, nor treat as their children only their own children. A competent provision is secured for the aged till their death, employment for the middle-aged, and the means of growing up for the young. The widowers, widows, orphans, childless men, and those who are disabled by disease, are all sufficiently maintained.

Each man has his rights, and each woman her individuality safeguarded. They produce wealth disliking that it should be thrown upon the ground, but not wishing to keep it for their own gratification. Disliking idleness they labor, but not alone with a view to their own advantage. In this way, selfish schemings are repressed and find no way to rise. Robbers, filchers, and rebellious traitors do not exist. Hence the outer doors remain open, and are not shut. This is the state of what I call the Great Similarity. (Miles Dawson, *Ethics of Confucius*. New York, 1915, p. 20.)

Read the Great Similarity as the New Deal or the Great Society, and the ideal Confucian vision emerges with lively liberal tinctures that contrast sharply with the dull shades of the tiresome conformism with which it has been associated in the Occidental mind. The political ideal of the Master turns out to be not an empire but a republic with a social-democratic program of government intervention for the good of the many.

Of course, it was not that side of the democratic ideological spectrum that ultimately prevailed in imperial China but the "conservative" one—that one captured in the Reaganesque aphorism that the central government is "part of the problem and not the solution." We have seen that Chinese central government, the splendorous imperial court in Peking, to have been more of a cultural than a government center. Durant, summing it up in 1934, presages a Reaganesque utopia in Churchillian terms: "If the best government is that which governs least, then the Chinese have had the best. Never has a government governed so many people, or governed them so little, or so long." (Durant, p. 796.)

When the Manchus fell in 1911 and China had its chance at

republican democracy on the national level, Mukerjee predicted that

the idea of a Chinese parliament, which may unite in its membership the various contending factions, will remain the fabric of a dream until the local democratic institutions are applied to the national government and the foreign institutions adapted to the peculiar needs and traditions of the different provinces. (Mukerjee, p. 183.)

The democracy posters in Peking and the Taiwanese fighters for democratic independence indeed appear to be able to lay good claim to Confucian ethical origins for their instincts for democracy.

9 The Hills Are Alive

In Chapter 1, we saw that, historically, barbarism and civilization were realities that have existed side by side and not necessarily in sequence. The same may be said of autocracy and democracy in original societies. An outstanding anthropological field of study for this kind of coexistence has been the hill tribes of Burma and of the neighboring Indian State of Assam.

Before the arrival of the British, there had been authentic monarchies among the Shans and the Burmese, the two main racial divisions of Burma. The monarchs themselves were not absolute despots. The Burmese king, for example, could not make laws, only edicts which lapsed upon his death. He was bound by custom, which was the only accepted source of law, and could even be sued for civil wrongs.

Basically, the Burmese kingship was not hereditary. The king had to be elected by the previous king's council of ministers, following old tribal requirements for the election of each chieftain. Strong kings could make elections a mere formality; nevertheless, real elections took place during crises.

Because the Burmese regarded all men and women as being free and equal, there was no hereditary nobility along the lines of the British model. Local communities within reach of the royal authority were grouped together according to size and geography, but each village elected its leader, whose office was then formalized by royal appointment.

Having sanctioned local elections, how much did the king interfere in local decision-making? The answer from British anthropologist E. R. Leach sounds almost verbatim to that of historians de la Costa and Durant (see Chapter 1):

It is entirely consistent with the ideas about kingship current in both Shan and Burmese society that the successful, economically powerful, leader should himself disdain to take an active part in day-to-day administrative affairs. Such practical matters are for underlings; the king himself should live apart in his palace surrounded by his numerous wives and concubines. (E. R. Leach, *Political Systems of Highland Burma*. London: G. Bell and Sons, Ltd., 1954, p. 189.)

Thus, as in India and China, Kachin villages were left free to develop their own indigenous patterns of government. In the process they managed to prove the corollary of the Chestertonian assertion of the coexistence of barbarism and civilization—the simultaneous undertaking in the same region of autocracy and democracy. The Kachins called these the *gumsa* and the *gumlao*, respectively.

Along with Leach, two other British anthropologists, H. N. C. Stevenson and J. H. Hutton, have found contrasting types of community government in the hills of Burma. Stevenson found autocracy among the Chins of Falam and Haka and democracy among the Chins of Tiddim. (See H. N. C. Stevenson, *The Hill Peoples of Burma*. London: Longmans, Green, 1968). Hutton discovered that some communities among the Sema and the Konyak were democratic, but others were quite the reverse. (See J. H. Hutton, *The Sema Nagas*. London: Oxford University Press, 1968.)

In the local Jinghpaw language the contrast is represented in the terms *gumsa* and *gumlao* (Leach, p. 198). The *gumsa* are regarded as ruled by chiefs who come from a hereditary aristocracy; the *gumlao* reject all hereditary class differences.

There are a variety of explanations about the origin of these contrasting systems. One version traces the deviation to not earlier than the turn of the century when a spirit of republicanism manifested itself... among certain tribesmen who found the yoke of the Duwa [a hill tribe] irksome and were impatient of control, [and] declared themselves *kumlao* or rebels, threw off their hereditary connection with the Duwa, and settled themselves in solitary villages of their own. (Leach, p. 199.)

However, Leach notes that the word *gumlao* is mentioned in an English source as early as 1828. Burmese author Kawlu Ma Nawng places the origin of the *gumlao* movement as early as 400 years ago. (Leach, p. 199.)

In any case, the British, resorting to their old Indian policy of discouraging indigenous democratic institutions, set their face against this Burmese republican movement and refused to recognize the *gumlao*. Nevertheless, this native democratic structure survived up to as late as 1954 when Leach observed that "in the majority of present-day Jinghpaw-speaking *gumlao* communities, the 'republicanism' appears to be quite genuine." (Leach, p. 201.)

Stevenson gives some detail on the workings of this original tribal democracy.

> Prior to the Annexation [by the British], the Zanniat and the Tashon were democratic tribes whose villages were ruled by councils of elders (called *Nam Kap*) selected to represent village quarters or in some cases patrilineal extended families.... These I have labeled the Democratic Group. The remainder were ruled by headmen from time immemorial, and I have called the Autocratic Group." (H. N. C. Stevenson, *The Economics of the Central Chin Tribes*. Bombay: The Times of India Press, n.d., p. 14.)

There were headmen in the democratic communities, but they had "no traditional backing," which "in practice means that in all their doings they lean more heavily on their councils than do the Autocratic headmen." (Stevenson, *Economics*, p. 16.)

These village councils, called *klangpi*, possessed powers almost coextensive with those of the headmen and had to be consulted on "any important work." To be a councillor (*klangsuak*) one had to be an outstanding person and a "feast giver," paralleling what we shall see to be a crucial item on the "campaign agenda" for councillors in the South Sea islands—not too far removed from political party picnics in Western-oriented democracies.

Stevenson also contrasts some of the Chin tribes and the Lushai-Kuki tribes which have hereditary tribal chiefs and a political aristocracy with "a large number of the central and southern Chin tribes [which] were ruled, in pre-annexation days, by democratic political organizations." (Stevenson, *Hill Peoples*, p. 7.)

"Each village of the democrats," he writes, "had its own council, members of which were elected to represent either the main families in the village, or the residential quarters, or the vested interests of the feast-givers; and each was virtually autonomous." (Stevenson, *Hill Peoples*, p. 7.)

The autocracy/democracy variation is present also among the tribes designated as Naga, whose region straddles Burma and the Indian State of Assam. A political scientist who is a native of the region, Mashangthei Horam, scrutinizes specific tribes in the group and finds that the Konyaks follow an autocratic "kingship"; the Angamis have no chiefs "worth the name," their villages "being held together by an extremely loose form of democracy." The Tangkhul have chiefs "with a great deal of authority," whereas the Aos "are more democratic minded though they too have a tradition of village chieftainship." (Mashangthei Horam, *Naga Polity*. Delhi: B. R. Publishing Corp., 1975, p. 85.)

Where there are chiefs the procedure for election is remarkably free of arbitrariness. Horam describes its simple features:

A meeting of all the adult males of the village (women never attend such meetings) [note—some Swiss Cantons today still indulge in the same sexist exclusion] is held on the village green. They usually assemble without much ado as the selection of a Chief affects every one of them. The selection of the First Man of the village ought to be and is a serious business and therefore carefully done. There is no secrecy in the method of selection. But even before the meeting is held, the candidature of a certain person is almost certain. It has already been discussed around the family hearths, on the way to the fields, in the village sitting-out places and certainly during the gossip hours. (Horam, pp. 74–75.)

Thus, the candidate for chieftainship is, by virtue of his outstanding personal qualities, the unofficial but unanimous choice of almost the entire village. Thus, when the selection meeting takes place, the elders of the different clans, after a certain amount of discussion, come to the point and suggest the name.

There are general murmurs of assent all around—and at times perhaps of dissent but drowned in the general hubbub—and the selection is over. The meeting disperses but not before the date, time and venue of the ceremony to invest the new Chief are decided upon by the Village Priest and other elders. (Horam, p. 75.)

The qualifications for candidacy are not very different from those expected of a U.S. Republican or Democrat: "Good physique, dominating personality, eloquence in speech, bravery on the battlefield and kindness of heart." (Horam, p. 74.)

The chief's power is circumscribed by rules that provide for his removal in case of dishonesty, lapse of duty, despotism, or general inefficiency. He must also consult with the village council, whose members are elected to give representation to all the clans residing in the village and which provides a "fairly effective constitutional check on the powers of a Chief especially if he is over-ambitious for himself." (Horam, p. 74.)

The village council is not just a consultative body. It performs executive, administrative, and judicial functions, and its meetings are neither perfunctory nor frivolous. Horam contrasts the serious tone of their meetings with those of the larger "all-village" reunions which "prove to be full of loud and heated arguments dotted with bursts of laughter" and are "more often than not inconclusive and time-consuming." (Horam, p. 85.)

To ensure seriousness of purpose, the number of members of the village council are kept at a minimum, normally between nine and thirty, with the members holding prior meetings with their own clans "to get the facts of the case before coming to the meetings of the Village Council." The councillors' term of office varies from tribe to tribe. Among the Aos the term is three to five years. Among the Tangkhuls the councillor keeps office as long as he retains the confidence of the clan he represents. However, the office is never hereditary. (Horam, p. 86.)

Colonial policy has been perceived as responsible for introducing hereditary succession in chieftainships. In Phuncham village, the chieftainship of which belongs to author Horam's clan, the village elders (including the author's father) recall that it was the British who imposed hereditary chiefs "to guarantee a stable administration from their point of view." (Horam, p. 76.)

We saw the British perform this kind of excising operation on the native democracy in village India. We shall see it done by the Spaniards in the Philippines where they transformed the consensual *datu*, the chief of the original independent settlements, into Spanish-appointed and hereditary *cabezas de barangay* representing the will not of their people but of the Spanish governor-general in Manila and, ultimately, of the Spanish king in Madrid.

Despite all this, the hills of Burma are alive with the original democracy.

10 The *Adat*—Durable Cake

The Malay race today dominates an extended peninsula and thousands of islands in Southeast Asia. They populate Indonesia, Malaysia, the Philippines, and Brunei, and they are an important minority in Thailand and Singapore. Their seafaring sweep also took them thousands of miles westward across the Indian Ocean to the African island of Madagascar, where they combined with black races to produce the current unique, social formation of the Malagasy Republic.

Several massive cultural waves have washed ashore the sprawling Southeast Asian region, leaving valuable sedimentary traditions that have enriched Malay civilization. The most pervasive imprints are those made by Hinduism and Islam. Except for the Philippine Archipelago, where the ubiquitous Spanish stone church is the universal monument of the prevailing Catholic culture, the visible marks of the popular culture in the rest of the region are shaped in the architecture of the Hindu subcontinent and the Muslim Middle East.

But the Malay race does have a history that predates the advent of Hinduism, Islam, and Christianity, and beneath these thick and ornate imported overlays there is perceptible and operational, even today, the stubborn structure of the original customary law.

The Hinduized emperors in Java and Sumatra, the Muslim sultans who later took over large sections of those islands and other territories including the Malay Peninsula, and the Dutch and the British governors—all had to come to terms with the obstinate "cake of custom." What gives both leavening and substance to this cake is the *adat*, the Malay customary law which was developed before the Christian era, almost a millennium in advance of the Anglo-Saxon common law which originated under Alfred the Great in the ninth century.

Indonesian author and educator S. Takdir Alisjahbana vests the *adat* with wider and deeper meaning than current concepts of custom and convention, embracing "everything we call law [as well as] economics, politics and the arts." (S. Takdir Alisjahbana, *Indonesia*. London: Oxford University Press, 1975, p. 33.)

Administering the *adat* was the principal duty of the village government, composed of a headman elected from the descendants of the oldest branch of the tribe, as well as a council of elders. The village communities were "rather like miniature democratic republics," and the headman and council arrived at important decisions "by collective deliberation. Naturally in a democracy of this type, in which a premium is put on unanimity of opinion, the position of the *balai* [community meeting place] was extremely important." (Alisjahbana, p. 34.) The deliberations were called *musyawarah* and the consensus *mufakat*.

Decisions arrived at by consensus are not imposed from above or from the outside and are completed only after everyone concerned has had an opportunity to participate, assert, and object. In this absence of arbitrariness, the procedure partakes of a genuinely democratic character.

To the Westerner who has been accustomed to the adversarial method of yeas and nays, such a "no victors and no vanquished" system is not easy to accept as democratic. However, an increasing number of Western observers are suggesting that consensus replace voting in certain areas and levels of popular discussion.

Admittedly, such a consensual process would be impractical in national, state, provincial, or even municipal elections and referenda. Even the direct voting democracy of the early Greek city-states, duplicated in today's Swiss cantons, is not practical for Switzerland's parliamentary elections. But the fact that consensual as well as direct (as opposed to representative) democracies are not useful above certain levels and areas does not make either of these practices less democratic.

Distinguished American diplomat Harlan Cleveland has proposed that decision-making by consensus replace adversarial voting in the United Nations. He concedes that the proposal may sound visionary but

only to Americans and Europeans who have grown up in the belief that parliamentary procedure and Robert's "Rules" are the very stuff of democracy.... that is a minority view in the modern world, and even in the West is a rather recent notion, not deeply rooted in classical or Christian thought. Consensus is practiced in Quaker meetings, in a modern Western family, and in British and American trial juries. ... [and] it will not seem strange to a Japanese businessman, a Chinese scholar, an African villager. (Harland Cleveland, "The U.S. vs. the U.N.?" The *New York Times Sunday Magazine*, May 4, 1975, p. 13.)

Pursuing the broad lines of this proposal, a "Symposium on Traditional Governance in Non-Western Cultures" was held in February, 1980, at the East-West Center in Hawaii under the sponsorship of the Charles F. Kettering Foundation. Participants from Asia, the Pacific Islands, and the United States read papers on indigenous decision-making practices among the Maoris, Japanese, Chinese, Western Samoans, and Indians. The declared objective of the meeting was to explore the applicability of these non-Western methods to management and policy development in Western or Westernized societies. The common characteristic found among these samplings was the element of consensus as opposed to adversarial decisions.

Some critical comment was made on the inapplicability of consensus-making to heterogenous societies, since the process requires acceptance of common norms and values. However, no one doubted the absence of arbitrariness or dictation in the practice. Thus, a consensual society was viewed, per se, as a substantive democracy. (William P. Shaw and Edwin P. McLain, "Learning from the Past/Lessons for the Future." Symposium on Traditional Governance in Non-Western Cultures, Charles F. Kettering Foundation, 1981, p. 12.) In the Malay culture, the *adat* was both the foundation for consensus and "the regulator of political and legal affairs." (N. J. Ryan, *The Cultural Heritage of Malaya*. Singapore: Longman, 1973, p. 43.) The assertion by historians like de la Costa that customary law, whether in Europe or Asia, provided the traditional hedge against centralized despotism is reiterated of the *adat* by N. J. Ryan: "*Adat* had bound everyone and had been a bulwark against tyranny by chiefs and rulers." (Ryan, p. 43.) The advent of Hinduized empires and Islamic sultanates began to erode this bulwark as "autocratic rule increased so that gradually a type of feudalism consisting of an aristocracy and a tied peasantry replaced the older, more democratic equality of the village." (Ryan, p. 43.)

The tenacious resistance to centralized rule by the upholders of the *adat* produced a compromise—a split, as it were—in the personality of the *adat* into the *adat perpateh* for the village community and the *adat temenggong* for larger communities. The former

regulated the life of a village community with as little repression as possible, for in small communities wrongs could best be settled by discussions and there were no crimes so serious that the community itself could not solve them in its own way. [Thus,] *adat perpateh* was an ideal system in such conditions for it was, above all, humane and personal, fraternal and democratic.

Adat temenggong began to change much of this emphasis for it was more suitable for larger communities and more complicated societies. ... The ruler and the ruling class became the administrators of the law and the rest of the people its recipients. The social system was less democratic and more authoritarian. (Ryan, pp. 47–48.)

Some authors, such as British historian R. J. Wilkinson, play down the differences between these two forms of *adat*. As if to stress the democratic character of the original law, Wilkinson wrote in 1908 that "the *adat temenggong* was the *adat perpateh* administered on autocratic lines." (R. J. Wilkinson, *Malay Law—An Introductory Sketch, Papers on Malay Subjects*. Kuala Lumpur: Federated Malay States Government Printer, 1908,

p. 5.). Others, like P. E. de Josselin de Jong, believe that the two terms might be anglicisms and not Malay concepts at all. (J. M. Gullick, *Indigenous Political Systems of Western Malaya*. London: The Athlone Press, 1965).

In any case, *adat perpateh* is said to have crossed over from the Minangkabau in Sumatra to the State of Negri Sembilan, where it flourished unchallenged until the installation of the first sultanate there in 1780. It was in other Malay states like Perak and Selangor, where Malacca-style sultanates had ruled since the early fifteenth century, that the *adat temenggong* appears to have first developed.

The *adat* confrontation was not a serious problem in the Philippine Archipelago, where Hindu culture washed over only lightly and Islamic sultanates were implanted only in select areas of the southern islands. There, in the sixteenth century, "the Spanish came to an area of Southeast Asia in which authority was for the most part exercised over small communities without any central direction." (Milton Osborne, *Southeast Asia*. London: George Allen & Unwin, 1979, p. 45.)

"Nothing about the early Filipinos," writes Horacio de la Costa, "struck the Spaniards more forcibly, coming as they did from a Europe of centralized monarchies, than that they had no kings." (Horacio de la Costa, S.J., *Readings in Philippine History*. Manila: La Solidaridad Publishing House, 1967.) The people lived in small, scattered settlements called *barangays*, after the name of the sailing vessels on which their ancestors had originally landed on their shores. Their chiefs were called *datus*, and most of the time there were "much more important considerations in the choice of a chief than blood." (De la Costa, p. 3.)

De la Costa cites the sixteenth-century Jesuit Father Colin, who describes one way that a humble villager might rise to chiefdom: "A man may be of lowly birth, but if he exerts himself, if by dint of hard work he accumulates wealth ... such a man acquires ascendancy and renown ... and the title [of chief] is conferred on him not by anyone superior to himself but solely by his own ability and prowess." (De la Costa, p. 3.) The description might well have come out of a leadership development manual of the U.S. Republican Party!

Becoming a *datu* did not ensure a good life for a man's kin. "It availed them nothing," asserts Father Colin, "that their parents and kinsmen were men of rank. And so it has happened that a man who was chief would have a son or brother a slave; and even worse than this, a slave of his own brother." (De la Costa, p. 4.)

In a subsequent chapter we shall see how the Spanish conquistador inevitably and rashly applied European feudal standards in assessing the Aztec civilization in Central America. In what the Spaniards were then about to baptize Filipinas (the Philippines), they did the same thing. Friar Juan de Plasencia, "in describing the social structure of the Tagalog *barangay*, fell easily into the language of Spanish feudalism":

> Besides the chiefs, who may be considered as composing the nobility, there were three estates: gentlemen, commoners, and slaves.
> The gentlemen were free men and were called *maharlicas*. They paid neither tax nor tribute to the *datu*, but were bound to follow him to war with their own weapons and gear...
> The commoners were called *aliping namamahay*. They are householders who serve a lord—whether it be the *datu* or someone else—with half the yield of the farm... and they row for him when he has a mind to set out to sea....
> The slaves are called *aliping saguigilir*, who serve the lord in his house and farm; these can be sold. (De la Costa, p. 4.)

Latter-day scholarship has tended to dismiss this allusion to feudal class distinction in early Filipino society as mostly romantic myth. In one of his last works, the late Dr. Robert Fox, one of the most respected Philippine anthropologists, wrote

> the fundamental characteristics of pre-Spanish social and political organization preclude as meaningful expressions such terms as "king," "noble," "slaves," "baranganic federations," and so forth. These ambiguous terms contribute to a myth building not consistent with analytic scholarship. (Robert Fox, *The Philippines in Pre-Historic Times*. Manila: Unesco National Commission of the Philippines, 1959, p. 32.)

"The problem lies," he adds, "in that many of the descriptions of early Spanish historians are of the few large communities which had just developed into trading centers with an atypical political structure due primarily to late Bornean and Muslim influences." (Fox, p. 33.)

Fox offers a simple outline of the early Filipino community as a democratic society:

> Leadership and authority was vested in the hands of family heads and older persons who were well-versed in customary laws and sanctions. These elders met together to settle disputes, as in the case of a divorce or of aggression or violence. Their decisions were actually a consensus of opinions in which the participants involved were represented and defended by kinsmen. Arguments were based on a developed customary law and the consensual decisions were reinforced by ritual sanctions. (Fox, p. 33.)

In the Muslim south the customary law retained its identity as the *adat*. Elsewhere the term was not as well known, but the substance of the customary law remained the same. Even to proud Spanish eyes, such as those of Miguel de Loarca, it looked like a respectable body of laws: "Their polity and laws, which, for barbarians, were not so very barbarous, consisted entirely of traditions and usages which they kept so strictly that they did not even admit the possibility of their being broken." (De la Costa, p. 5.)

Except in the stubborn southern Muslim areas of the Philippines, the *datu* as an institution would suffer the fate of other village chiefdoms which lost their independence at the hands of the British in the Indian subcontinent, the French in Africa, and the Spaniards in the New World. The *datu* would be renamed *cabeza de barangay* (*head of barangay*), transformed into an hereditary officer representing not his people but the Spanish governor at the capital in Manila, his heirs later to form a species of privileged class called the *principalia*, intruding thus into the original democracy with an alien social stratification.

Thousands of miles to the west the original institution of the Malay village chief would more successfully resist a determined but less thorough Europeanization and centralization by the French colonial government.

"The five million people of the Malagasy Republic came across the Indian Ocean from the islands of Indonesia," writes anthropologist Peter J. Wilson. They now have African blood but "the Malagasy language bears out the people's Indonesian origins, for it is distinctly Malayo-Polynesian and seems most closely related to Maanjan, a language of Borneo." (Peter J. Wilson, *Natural History*, December, 1977, p. 13.)

The French took over Madagascar in the 1890s and immediately set out to reorganize and centralize the government. French-appointed district officers were sent out of the capital to exact cooperation, work, and taxes from the provincial areas, a function inherited by the appointees of the current independent Malagasy government.

Wilson lived for one year with the Tsimihety tribe, one of whose proud distinctions is that it produced the first president of the Malagasy Republic, Philibert Tsiranana. Another distinction of the Tsimihety is their fierce egalitarianism: "Every village is a voluntary confederacy of households," Wilson observes, "each has an equal say in local affairs exercised through the universal Malagasy institution of *fokon'olona* [people's council or village assembly] which is presided over by the village elders." (Wilson, p. 33.) "Of course, the French and the Malagasy government after them have tried to govern the Tsimihety." (Wilson, p. 33.) In emulation of the Spaniards who in the Philippines had renamed the consensual *datu cabeza de barangay* and transformed him into an appointed representative of Spanish authority, the French gave the village headman the Gallic title *chef de village* and made his an appointed office along with other *quartiers* (district) officials.

However, the central government appointees are regarded as little more than ceremonial officers. "The Tsimihety have little choice but to accept these formalities," Wilson recalls, but "at the same time they have found ways to avoid this structure for all practical purposes and thereby preserve their democracy." (Wilson, p. 33.)

An earlier study of original Malagasy democracy is provided by anthropologist Ralph Linton of the University of Wisconsin. As part of a Marshall Field Expedition to Madagascar in 1926, Linton researched the indigenous government structure of the

Tanala (People of the Forest), one of the principal tribal groups in the eastern part of the island. (See Ralph Linton, *The Tanala, a Hill Tribe of Madagascar.* Chicago: Field Museum of Natural History, Pub. 317, Anthropological Series, vol. XXII.)

As Wilson would later discover of the Tsimihety in 1977, Linton found the *fokon'olona* among two of the tribe's divisions, the Menabe and the Ikongko, settling "matters of general policy, internal disputes and minor criminal cases." Some informants told Linton that the council was limited to the Notables, the French title applied to the "important men" of each village, others that it included the entire adult male population. However, "the distinction is not an important one," Linton writes, "for the meetings were always public and all villagers, including women, had the right to speak." Again, the procedure was consensual: "The matter was threshed out until it was felt that the whole group was in agreement." (Linton, p. 111.)

The council meetings were called *kabary*, which Linton claims to be an equivalent of the term "palaver," a word of Portuguese extraction which we shall encounter often in looking into the traditional democratic practices of continental Africa. Linton describes it as "a generic term for meetings, discussions, speeches, etc." (Linton, p. 111.)

Linton discovered, particularly among the Ikongko, "a well-developed legal system with a concept of law similar to our own." (Linton, p. 111.) It is probable that this body of laws was descended from the *adat* of the original Malays who had come across the Indian Ocean in the fifth and sixth centuries.

Both the Menabe and Ikongko elected their chiefs, reserving the right to depose them at will. Linton noted that "under French control the office of Andriambavety [Menabe chief] has been retained and its powers and its responsibilities considerably increased." (Linton, p. 111.) He became an agent of the French instead of a representative of his people. "He must provide the quotas of men demanded by the government for forced labor," and he could no longer "be deposed by the village without [French] government consent." (Linton, p. 112.)

Linton visited Madagascar during French rule, Wilson after the inauguration of the independent Malagasy Republic. The expert observations by both men constitute still one more rebuke to those who have accepted without question the popular notion that Asian or African substantial democracy must be a Western transplant. Here is a Malayo-African race succeeding in protecting its original democracy from Western colonial impositions.

Wilson recounts the almost mocking procedure by which "an instruction from a district officer" is received by the village assembly. The *chef de village*, "hilariously imitating the district officer," announces the instruction to the village assembly. After the laughter has subsided, the senior elders initiate serious discussion, which most of the time ignores the subject of the district officer's instructions.

British common law originated in the Middle Ages in the decisions of local courts. Malay customary law was born in village councils. Ultimately, both of them came from the people, from human beings, uncoerced, bound only by the moral compulsion of their own free will. In one form or another, this human custom of acting as free men and women developing their own free traditions will cross our path again and again as we move across the Pacific, into the New World, and over to the old kingdoms of black Africa.

11 Stone Age Legislatures

In the Central Asaro Valley of the Eastern Highlands of New Guinea there is a group of tribes anthropologists identify as the Gahuku-Gama. They share the same language and culture, some of whose unique characteristics have attracted special research.
University of Washington anthropologist K. E. Read has examined "two largely antithetical orientations" in the culture—the values of "strength" and "equivalence." (K. E. Read, "Leadership and Consensus in a New Guinea Society." *The Anthropologist*, vol. 61, 1959, p. 35.) "Equivalence" is expressed in maxims that bear striking resemblance to the Golden Rule of Western Christendom, i.e., "do not injure a fellow clansman," "be ready to make redress for a wrong done" and "be moderate in your manner of treating others." (Read, p. 35.)
In earlier days, "equivalence" also controlled traditional intertribal feuding which today has been largely replaced by soccer matches. The value dictates that no team should be allowed to establish its outright superiority and emerge as the final victor. Therefore, "games usually go on for days until the scores are considered to be equal." (Read, p. 35.)
"Strength," on the other hand, expects to be aggressive, a warrior "included to swagger and boast." However, his strength must manifest itself also in oratory. He must "be able to express himself with force and also [be] knowledgeable in various pre-

scriptive speeches which are required for different occasions." (Read, p. 36.) It is here that the two apparently contradicting values find valuable congruence.

The most important occasions for the display of oratorical skills are the "gatherings," assemblies at which every member of the segments involved is entitled to be present and participate in the discussions. These gatherings are either spontaneous, mostly those called for quick judicial settlement, or formally convened for more serious deliberations on clan activities.

The decisions express the consensus of the gathering, counting on the expectation of "equivalence" that a man "should be amenable to persuasion [and] any matter which concerns the tribe or its segments should be decided freely on the basis of arrived consensus." (Read, p. 36.)

The clan orator opens the proceedings and "launches into a speech which is partly a panegyric upon himself and partly a sermon in which he may stress such group values as restraint, cooperation, and friendship." (Read, p. 36.) These are virtues descended from "equivalence," and it is the clan orator with his "strength" who must see to it that they are practiced. Yet, while he is expected to retain "a measure of control over these gatherings," this control is "the more subtle and perhaps the more difficult to maintain because he cannot enforce a decision." (Read, p. 36.) Only the collective assembly can enforce its consensus.

Thus, the two antithetical values converge to produce an exercise that is remarkably free of coercion—a genuinely democratic function. The clan orator emerges as a figure comparable to, but less powerful than, the eloquent modern prime minister, who is limited by his parliament, his party, and the laws and values of his constituency.

Farther south, anthropologists Frazer and Rivers, studying the Australian aborigines, found that "these savages are ruled neither by chiefs nor kings" and that "so far as their tribes can be said to have a political constitution, it is a democracy." Likening their deliberative assembly to a senate, Frazer and Rivers noted that the old men, meeting in council, "decide on all measures of importance, to the practical exclusion of younger men," a feature reminiscent of the senior composition of the current British House of Lords. (Robert W. Williamson, *The Social and Political Systems of Central Polynesia*. London: Cambridge University Press, 1924, vol. 1, pp. 374–75.)

New Guinea was once described by a nineteenth century traveler as the land that all time had passed by, while the Australian aborigines have been regarded as the most visible living throwbacks to the Stone Age. If all that be true, if the Gahuku-Gama and the aborigines are, indeed, original, untouched human societies, then we have here one more reason for stripping the caricatured caveman of his despotic club and rating the humor of the Flintstones as sick.

Across the Tasman Sea from the island continent of Australia is that southwestern gateway to Polynesia, New Zealand, 10 percent of whose population is of Maori descent. Millennia before the waters of the South Seas had ever been given those European names and their many island races baptized with the generic Greek designation Polynesia, the Maoris had settled what is now New Zealand after crisscrossing the ocean along with their sister nations in the Great Migration. When the British colonized the twin islands in the late 1800s, they discovered a society with a complex system of tribal government. (Neville Baker, "Notes on Some Maori Governance Patterns Upon Which Western Management May Draw." Kettering Symposium, p. 12.)

Some apparently inconsistent terms were applied descriptively to Maori society by early British travelers. Eldson Best, in an account reprinted by the New Zealand Government in 1974, called the Maoris at once "communistic," "theocratic," and "democratic." (Eldson Best, *The Maori As He Was*. Wellington: A. R. Shearer Government Printer, 1974, pp. 93–97.)

They were communistic because they gave preeminence to the interests of the community; theocratic because they had evolved a "substitute for civil law"—certain "restrictive regulations" called the *tapu*, which they believed to be sanctioned by their gods; and democratic because they practiced "public discussion of all proposals and activities." (Best, pp. 93–97.)

The three-tiered tribal organization was founded on the *whanau*, or extended families, which formed the *hapu*, or clans, which formed the *iwi*, or tribe. There was open discussion on all levels, the *whanau* among themselves, the *hapu* among family groups, and the *iwi* among the clans.

These meetings were held on the *marae*, which, in pre-European times, was the focal point of the Maori community. The *marae* was "an open space in the village for meeting, hospitality, and discussion, for celebrating life, preparing for war, and grieving the dead." (Baker, Kettering Symposium, p. 8.)

"Western man relies on force," reads Baker's notes, "but in contrast to this, [it was] the Maori gods [that] preserved order, and fear of their anger was the most powerful influence in the Maori commune." (Baker, Kettering Symposium, p. 8.) Thomas Jefferson had only one "Nature's God" to invoke in his Declaration, but the Maoris have a hierarchy of deities to call upon and fear—Io, the Supreme Being; various "departmental" and "district" gods; as well as "inferior beings" which were deified ancestors and local demons. Together they ensure Maori order in a way that Jefferson's impersonal spirit of Nature could not. Thus, the statutory laws of Jeffersonian democracy had in the end to be implemented by force. Maori law was enforced by mutual consent.

Recognizing the persistent validity and utility of indigenous Maori democratic institutions, the New Zealand Government has begun, according to Baker, "to reinstitute town hall type meetings similar to Maori practice, in which citizens can discuss critical decisions that affect their everyday lives." (Baker, Kettering Symposium, p. 9.)

As we move out across the South Seas to the capitals of other island nations, we shall see order maintained by policemen dressed as New York patrolmen in Samoa, London bobbies in Fiji, and French *poilu* in Tahiti, but in their villages the Polynesian counterparts of the Maori voluntary democracy will inevitably come to be viewed as living and stubborn monuments to the universality and originality of the democratic ideal.

12 The Consensual Islands

In 1791, the British naval ship *Pandora*, scouring the South Seas for the *Bounty* mutineers, stumbled upon a seventeen-square-mile volcanic island called Rotuma, which today forms part of Fiji. The British tars came away with impressions of an all-powerful chief or king ruling the island, but latter-day scholarship tells a different story.

The Rotuma chief or *sou* was not a hereditary king but was elected from different districts every six months, extendible to twenty months. Gardiner writes that the *sou* had little to do with actual governing, "and, though he reigned, he had no authority, his chief duty being to get fat!" (Gardiner, *J. A. I.*, vol. XXVII, p. 460.) Indeed, the figure of the ruling but nongoverning chief or king looms large and omnipresent all over the bounding waters of Polynesia. *Le roi regne, il ne gouverne pas*—so goes the apt Gallic phrase cited by Robert Williamson in his three-volume work. (Robert W. Williamson, *The Social and Political Systems of Central Polynesia*. London: Cambridge University Press, 1924, p. 27.)

South Seas political systems were seen as despotic or democratic, depending on the owner of the beholding eye. The more preemptory investigations by European explorers and discoverers, as noted by Williamson (vol. 3, p. 125), yielded uniform deductions of despotism. But more democratically oriented American naval officers visiting the Society Islands in the early nineteenth century viewed the local political scene with a more liberal beholding eye: "On some of the islands there are kings, but the rank is mainly nominal, though tribute is paid to them by the several towns over which their sway extends." The report also noted three classes in the male population: "the *neas* or *omatas*, who are the principal chiefs; the *katokas*, who are the landholders, not of noble birth; and the *kawas* or slaves." ("Report of the Voyage of the U.S. Exploring Squadron," Commanded by Captain Charles Wilkes of the United States Navy. Auburn: Alden, Beardsley & Company, 1852, p. 406.)

These different estates held public councils presided over by the oldest chief, and although "no regular vote is ever taken at these assemblages," nevertheless, "the opinion of the majority decides the subject matter under consideration." (Wilkes Report, p. 406.) A majority opinion without vote would seem to correspond to the consensual process we have seen practiced by the Maoris, as well as by most of the democratic communities in traditional Asia.

What the military eyes of the American naval officers perceived has been confirmed in later anthropological research—South Seas societies resembling less the classic Western despotisms than European limited monarchies and the American republic. Indeed, the more deliberate and discerning eye of the anthropologist has detected both despotism and democracy in the vast island region, confirming our original proposition that both these social conditions have coexisted and have not necessarily constituted a sequential evolution in human history. Yet, while there has been coexistence of the two conditions, one has appeared more to prevail as the general rule and the other the exception. The ruling executive has more often been either a nominal official, with the real power in the hands of a popular council, or one with real powers that have been severely limited, however, by popular consent.

Samoa is a useful model for this uneven coexistence. In *Rovings in the Pacific*, the Samoan islands are seen as "cut up into countless chieftainships, each chief possessing absolute power over his own district." (*Rovings in the Pacific*, 1851, vol. II, p. 158.) Stair saw chiefs of both sorts, some with "very limited powers" and others who used powers "in a very tyrannical manner." (Stair, p. 76.) Williamson writes of French missionaries who thought that "every Samoan village had chiefs who governed their subjects as they thought fit, or rather they hardly governed them, and the subjects did pretty much as they pleased." (Williamson, vol. 3, p. 101.)

There also appeared to have been genuine decentralization of government. Neither a chief nor a general council would interfere in the affairs of districts. The chief seemed to be important only in war, and "he would, owing to the system of local self-government, know little or nothing of the affairs of the districts or villages."

Williamson ascribes to the Samoan king and his chiefs, acting together, prerogatives in diplomatic negotiations, which "would presumably be great." Like the American president, they would conduct dialogues and enter into "political intrigues" with other rulers without consulting the popular council until a definite proposition was ready to be put before it, much like an American president would present a treaty for ratification to the U.S. Senate only after he has negotiated and signed it.

On the other hand, "as regards administrative and parliamentary power, we have to bear in mind that the general weight of evidence appears to indicate that in most parts of Samoa the power of the chiefs as a class was subject to a greater or less amount of control by the *fono* [council] of the people or their representative." (Williamson, vol. 3, p. 115.)

On the island of Fotuna, north of Samoa, the king was selected from the heads of families, but he was not an absolute monarch. Before they had ever heard of the British parliamentary system, they had a legislative body that met from time to time.

S. I. Thomson would categorically characterize the institutions of the island of Niue as "republican." In ancient times the ruling power was held by the *toa* or fighting men, and "the party that happened to be in ascendant elected a king to be their mouth piece." This king governed "with the consent of the council which met in the open air once a month and carried out their decrees by the force of public opinion." (S. I. Thomson, cited by Williamson.)

This semblance of a party system emerges in sharper focus in the workings of the popular councils, particularly those of Samoa. It is these councils, in fact, that stamp the most indelible democratic marks on South Seas societies.

The almost uniform term applied to these councils in the whole region is *fono*, linguistically identical to the Maori *hono*, both terms meaning to "join together" or "unite." As among the Maoris, in the whole of Polynesia the meeting place is the village green, called the *marae*, usually facing an assembly or guest house called the *falatele*.

The village *fono* was composed of the heads of families, one of whom was like a prime minister to the chief. It was this prime minister who called the meeting, whose decision, whether legislative or judicial, was unappealable. Women and children were not allowed in the meeting house, and younger men were allowed only to sit in front of it during the meeting. After the speeches were made and punishments for violations of law meted out, one of the *fono* members would make a speech to those outside, announcing the conclusions of the assembly and enjoining their observance.

The great *fono*, for a large or important district or division, or for all of Samoa, was attended with much more elaborate ceremony. The call was issued by the host village district through the *tulafale*, the superior class of clan orators who went about informing each village district about the meeting agenda. Each chief had his appointed place in the house or on the *marae*. Some writers refer to hereditary seats and ancestral stone benches on the *marae*. The leading orator of the host village was the meeting chairman who delivered the opening speech, decided disputed points, made the summation, and adjourned the assembly.

While the opening speech was "greatly prolonged" by an intricate series of protocolar salutations to the other delegates, the regular speeches were expected to last no more than fifteen to twenty minutes. In the truly great assemblies, the *Ao tetele* or "the great honors," a special form of greeting, was directed to each village district, each island, each division, and to Samoa itself.

The *fono* decisions were called *tulafono*, or acts of council, arrived at by general consensus after prolonged discussion. While there was no voting reflecting relative strengths of political groupings, there appeared to have existed "strong" and "weak" parties. Williamson makes mention of the *malo* or strong party, whose position on various questions for discussion eventually prevailed over that of the *vaivai* or weak party. The latter, although unable to win the day in discussions, nevertheless, "retained their power within their respective districts." The *malo* was, in effect, the government party and the *vaivai* the loyal opposition, making for a precolonial system remarkably presaging that yet to be transplanted by the coming European colonizer.

The *fono* was a universal Polynesian institution, and on other islands it has been viewed by different writers in contrasting lights. Three authorities—Mariner, Thomson, and Radcliffe-Brown (cited by Williamson)—regard the *fono* in Tonga as totally autocratic, convened not to discuss problems but only to communicate orders by the chiefs. No discussion was allowed and "a chief held it whenever he had something to say to his people." However, Williamson prefers the testimony of others, such as West and Erskine, who insist that at least some of the Tongan *fono* "were deliberative assemblies, at which various people spoke, and which were, to this extent, comparable with the *fono* of Samoa." (Williamson, vol. 2, p. 480.) Furthermore, according to these latter two authorities, in both Samoa and Tonga the king was expected to consult the *fono* on important matters.

In Tahiti the popular assembly was not called *fono* but *apoo*. As in the *fono*, the principal speakers were the orators, but the *ra'atira*, or landowning middle class, appeared to have occupied a considerable portion of the discussion period. At least one author, Ellis, writes that the discussions were so intense that sometimes they ended not in harmonious understanding but in district warfare, rather like the more violent adjournments of the early British parliament and of the modern Japanese diet and Italian chamber of deputies.

Ellis, Foster, and Moerenhout attest to the *apoo* being more than a rubber stamp assembly. "They had to be consulted and persuaded, and seem to have had considerable freedom of speech... and it was generally necessary even for the king to introduce them into the discussion of any measure of importance." (Williamson, vol. 2, p. 485.) The fastidiously ceremonious convocation of a national assembly, reflecting the seriousness with which popular participation was enjoined in the *apoo*, is described in detail by Ellis as follows:

> As regards the summoning of the people, when a measure affecting all the inhabitants was adopted, the king's messenger was sent with a bundle of *niau* or leaflets. On entering a district, he went to the habitation of the principal chiefs and, presenting a coconut leaf, delivered the orders of the king. The acceptance of the leaf was a declaration of compliance with the requisition, and declining it was an intimation of hostility to the measure proposed.
>
> Hence the messenger, when he had travelled round the island, reported to the king who had received the leaflets and who had refused them. Chiefs who approved sent their own messengers to their respective tenants and dependents, with a coconut leaf for each and the orders of the king.
>
> This coconut leaf was the emblem of authority, and requisitions for property or labour, preparations for war or the convocation of a national assembly were made by sending the coconut leaf to those whose service or attendance was required. (Williamson, vol. 2, p. 487.)

In the Marquesas the independent electors of the valley of the Taipii people "were not to be brow-beaten by priests, chiefs, idols or devils," the people seemed to be governed by "a sort of tacit common sense law."

It was presumably this common sense law that invited interpretation and implementation by the people's "great assemblies," gatherings of the "chiefs of the bays and valleys." Williamson presumes that the not-to-be-brow-beaten electors would have been entitled to participate in these assemblies, although he proceeds with scholarly caution to admit to not being certain about "what classes of society may have been included in the term 'chiefs.'"

In Niue, where "republican institutions" flourished, there was a *fono* which was "half parliament, half law court." According to S.I. Thomson (cited by Williamson), "Nothing was too great or too small for its attention," and there was an effective, if amusing, way by which a village which refused to obey a *fono* decree was brought into line. "In [that] case, the next *fono* was held in the rebellious village; this meant a supply of food during the meeting, and the *fono* would then go on with its meetings until the refractory village submitted," a strategy of attrition reminiscent of the thirteenth-century citizens of Viterbo, Italy, who, after two years of fruitless waiting, forced seventeen assembled cardinals to make a decision on the next pope by sealing the palace, removing the roof, and reducing the cardinals' food supply to bread and water!

Finally, we return to Rotuma, where we originally found a king whose main function was to grow fat. The island was actually run by the *ngangaja*, or chiefs, who met in council to ascertain the wants of their people. The *pure*, or heads of families, had the power to reverse the action of the chiefs.

The consensual functions of the *fono* or *apoo* survive in the South Seas to this day. Harland Cleveland, describing its current version, points out that consensus is not necessarily equivalent to unanimity:

"Consensus" does not mean unanimous consent. In a Pacific island village, important decisions will draw all the villagers to a community circle, but only those who care about a particular decision will edge toward the circle's center to make their views known and their weight felt. The others will sit around the outside, often talking among themselves about something else. When the village elder is able to divine and announce the common view, that doesn't mean that everybody is an uncritical endorser of what will be done. It does mean that among those who water-buffaloes might be gored, there is at least passive acquiescence, and those who don't much care are willing to leave the outcome to those who do. To insist at this juncture, under Western procedures, that everyone's pulse be taken, and then to divide the converging company into clear yeas and nayes, would endanger the agreement already reached. (Harland Cleveland, "The U.S. vs. the U.N.?" The *New York Times Sunday Magazine*, May 4, 1975, p. 13.)

In the whole of Polynesia, the ancient government of Easter Island appears to have been the only one that was incurably despotic. Even there, however, the authority of the kings and chiefs gradually died away. Noted Yugoslav anticommunist dissident Mihajlo Mahajlov has warned that "right-wing dictatorships are the best fifth column for communist totalitarianism." Communism thrives on the anarchy that follows the collapse of dictatorships. On Easter Island, the collapse of the traditional dictatorship led to eventual anarchy.

Now a dependency of Chile as Isla de Pascua, the island awaits the restoration of Chilean constitutional government so that it might not slip into left-wing totalitarianism but instead experience at last that democracy which the rest of its sister South Sea islands have so early and so indigenously enjoyed.

13 Iroquois—the First American Republic

In the summer of 1983, I attended a gathering of the Seneca-Cayuga tribe in Grove, Oklahoma. There I met Minnie Thompson, then ninety-five years old, still hale and spry, so spry that she had not once missed her semiannual trip to Las Vegas to play the slot machines! Minnie told me she had been elected member of the tribal council ever since she could remember, that the council by the tribal rules was made up of twelve members, six male and six female.

A human rights activist recently observed in the current debate on what to do with undocumented foreigners in the United States: "The first illegal aliens in this country landed at Plymouth Rock in 1620!" While he was making a strong legal point, historically he was off the mark. The first undocumented aliens landed on the continent thousands of years ago, not from Europe but from Asia. They developed into many tribes and nations and eventually became known collectively by a combination of an Italian first name and Asian ethnic name mistakenly invoked by another Italian: American Indians.

A more challenging question for academic debate might read: "Which undocumented alien first brought democracy to America?"

In Chapter 8, I discussed a 1984 television documentary by the Public Broadcasting System in the United States showing the English colonists in Jamestown, Virginia, indulging in the undemocratic practice of class discrimination, the gentlemen eating under constructed shades with spoons and forks while the commoners had to eat with their hands in the broiling sun. A century later the third generation of those colonists would forge a radiantly democratic nation. "Fourscore and seven years" still later, one of its greatest chief executives would speak of it in an immortal address as "a new nation, conceived in liberty and dedicated to the proposition that all men are created equal."

However, American democracy was not born with the Declaration of Independence or the Constitution of the United States. Along with social inequality and, later, slavery, the colonists had been practicing "town hall democracy" for more than a century before finally rebelling against the English king. Some of them even had solemnized it in writing. On January 14, 1639, only nineteen years after the Plymouth landing, planters from Hartford, Wethersfield, and Windsor, small farming towns along the Connecticut River, met at Hartford and drew up the Fundamental Orders, setting up "one Public State or Commonwealth," with permanent limitations on government power, a representative system of government, the right to vote for all free men, and with no mention of the crown of England.

Yet, no matter how far in advance of its time the Hartford constitution may have appeared to be, it was not the first formal democracy in the New World.

Minnie Thompson's Seneca-Cayuga tribe in Oklahoma is descended from two Northeastern American nations, Seneca and Cayuga, which once formed part of the great Iroquois Confederacy. There were four other Iroquois tribes—the Mohawk, the Onondaga, the Oneida, and the Tuscarora. More detailed listings of Iroquois tribes note that "the entire Iroquoian people" were divided into three groups: "the first, the Iroquois, includes the Seneca, the Canada, the Mohawk, the Oneida, the Onondaga, the Cayuga, and the Susquehanna; the second includes the Nottaway and the Tuscarora; and the third, the Wyandot, includes the Hochelaga, the Huron, the Tionontati, the Neutral, and the Wenco." (Arlington Mallery and Mary Roberts

Harrison, *The Rediscovery of Lost America.* New York: E. P. Dutton, 1979, p. 57.)

Sometime in the first half of the fifteenth century, a council of wise men and chiefs of all the tribes, except the Tuscarora, met on the north shore of Lake Onondaga, near Syracuse in what is now upstate New York, and established a confederacy. (Lewis H. Morgan, *Ancient Society.* Cambridge: Belknap Press reprint, 1964, p. 113.) Other authors place the establishment of the confederacy on later dates, such as sometime in the closing decades of the sixteenth century. (See J. N. B. Hewitt, "A Constitutional League of Peace in the Stone Age of America," *Annual Report of the Board of Regents of the Smithsonian Institution, 1918.* Washington, D.C.: Government Printing Office, 1920.)

The democratic beginnings of the Iroquois Confederacy may be attributed to the character of the *ohwachira* (uterine family), one or more of which constituted the Iroquois matriarchal clan. Mothers and marriageable women in the clan had the traditional right to hold councils, particularly those for the nomination of candidates for chief and vice-chief, both of which could be nominated by mothers alone.

The council of women performed, among other functions, two which today would be identified as those of the right of initiative and the right of referendum. They had the right to formulate propositions for later discussion by the tribal council. They could also propose that the tribal council submit to the vote of all the people (including infants, whose mothers could cast their votes) "any question which might be occupying the attention of the council or the people." (Hewitt, p. 16.)

Hewitt lists among the rights of the clan that of

representation by one or more chiefs in the tribal council, to have its nomination for chief and subchief of the clan confirmed and installed by officers of the tribal council in earlier times, but since the institution of the league, by officers of the federal council, and that of the men or women, or both together, to meet in council. (Hewitt, p. 16.)

Some authors regard the vaunted democracy of the Iroquois as more apparent than real. Peter Farb, in an argument that

92 Will of the People

feminists could quickly assail as sexist, contends that the myth of Iroquois democracy is exploded by "scientific study" which reveals a disproportionate influence of women in the decision-making process! (See Peter Farb, *Man's Rise to Civilization as Shown by the Indians of North America from Primeval Times to the Coming of the Industrial State*. New York: E. P. Dutton, 1968.) The actual positions were held by men, such as that of *sachem*, or clan chief. However, Farb complains that "even though the women did not themselves rule, they had the sole power to appoint and to remove [the chiefs] from office." Farb describes the process of selection and dismissal:

The headwoman of the lineage assembled all the women of her household and her clan and discussed with them her choice for a successor *sachem*. Then she went to both moieties and got their approval. The women's control over the *sachem* did not end with his selection. If he failed to perform his duties as they liked, the headwoman gave him three stern warnings, after which he was removed and his badge of office given to a new candidate. (Farb, p. 77.)

Archeologist William M. Beauchamp, writing in 1906 for the New York State Education Department, recalled that the Jesuits credited "strange stories of the Iroquois...before they knew them better," such as the one about alternate male/female management:

The men and women there manage affairs alternately; so that if there is a man who governs them now, after his death it will be a woman, who during her lifetime will govern them in her turn except in what belongs to war; and after her death it will be a man who takes anew the management of affairs. (William M. Beauchamp, "Civil, Religious, and Mourning Councils and Ceremonies of Adoption of the New York Indians," *Bulletin* 113, *Archeology* 13, New York State Museum, 1906.)

In any case, the undeniable preeminence of the women among the Iroquois did not bother Lewis H. Morgan, who was more sanguine in his appreciation of the Iroquois political organization as the forerunner of the modern tripartite executive, legislative, and judicial system of government.

Morgan begins his analysis with the Iroquois *gens*, the consanguineous unit descended from a common ancestor. (He notes the consonance between the Latin *gens*, the Greek *yenos*, and the Sanskrit *ganas*, all signifying kin.) Each of the six Iroquois tribes were found to be composed of a maximum of eight *gentes*, named after members of the animal kingdom, i.e., Wolf, Bear, Turtle, Beaver, Deer, Snipe, Heron, and Hawk.

The *gens* individualized with a body of customary law, the *jus gentilicum*, as it were, providing for a list of ten basic rights, privileges, and obligations conferred and imposed upon its members:

1. The right of electing its *sachem* and chiefs.
2. The right of deposing its *sachem* and chiefs.
3. The obligation not to marry in the *gens*.
4. Mutual rights of inheritance of the property of deceased members.
5. Reciprocal obligations of help, defense, and redress of injuries.
6. The right of bestowing names upon its members.
7. The right of adopting strangers into the *gens*.
8. Common religious rites.
9. A common burial place.
10. A council of the *gens*.

(Morgan, p. 67.)

While election of the *sachem* was, in theory, by vote of both men and women, the choice was normally limited to a surviving male relative, and "usually fell upon a brother of the deceased *sachem*, or upon one of the sons of a sister." Despite this and other minor limitations, Morgan saw in the process of choice "the principle of democracy, which was born of the *gentes* [and] manifested itself in the retention by the *gentiles* of the right to elect their *sachems* and chiefs, in the safeguards thrown around the office to prevent usurpation, and in the check upon the election held by the remaining gentes." (Morgan, p. 71.)

Although the office of *sachem* was nominally for life, the tenure was practically during good behavior, since the council of the *gens*, as well as the tribal council, could depose him for misbehavior and loss of confidence. The council of the *gens*, writes Morgan, "was a democratic assembly because every adult male and female member had a voice upon all questions brought before it." (Morgan, p. 71.)

Playing down the heavy matriarchal hand detailed by Hewitt and lamented by Farb, Morgan says the council "elected and deposed its *sachems* and chiefs, elected keepers of the Faith, condoned or avenged the murder of a *gentilis*, and adopted persons into the *gens*." Whatever restrictions on free choice were imposed to respect matrilineal continuity, there was an obvious absence of that autocratic arbitrariness which is the mark of an undemocratic society, and Morgan perhaps was justified in his enthusiastic assessment that "all the members of an Iroquois *gens* were personally free," that "they were equal in privileges and in personal rights, the *sachems* and chiefs claiming no superiority," and that "liberty, equality, and fraternity, though never formulated, were cardinal principles of the gens." (Morgan, p. 71.)

The democracy of the Iroquois *gens* was duplicated and magnified in the tribe, which was composed of several *gentes*. The following characteristics and prerogatives distinguished the tribe:

1. The possession of a territory and a name.
2. The exclusive possession of a dialect.
3. The right to invest *sachems* and chiefs elected by the *gens*.
4. The right to depose these *sachems* and chiefs.
5. The possession of a religious faith and worship.
6. A supreme government consisting of a council of chiefs.
7. A head chief of the tribe in some instances.

(Morgan, p. 101.)

At the tribal level, the council seems to have been less under pressure by matriarchal privilege. Perhaps, Morgan is merely displaying a masculine bias when he concedes that "even the women were allowed to express their wishes and opinions [in the council] through an orator of their own selection ... but the decision was made by the council." Like the consensual process that we have seen prevailing in Asia and the South Seas, "unanimity was a fundamental law of its action among the Iroquois." However, Morgan cautions that "whether this usage was general I am unable to state." (Morgan, p. 105.)

The decisive feature is that the meetings of the council, which was composed of the elected chiefs of the *gentes*, were "open to any private individual who desired to address it on a public question." Thus, the council was an institution which provided the occasion for the practice of both representative and direct democracy.

The council deliberations appear to have received wondering praise from eyewitnesses. Beauchamp writes of "uniform courtesy in Iroquois debates," quoting a detailed account by Prof. Timothy Dwight, in his *Travels in New England and New York* (1822):

> When in council they spoke optionally; and listened to each speaker with a profound and very respectful silence; observing a decorum which might with great advantage be copied by our Congress, and your Parliament. When proposals for war or peace were made, or treaty proposed to them by the colonial governours, they met the ambassadours in council, and at the end of each part or proposition, the principal Indian delivered a short stick to one of his council as a token that it was his peculiar duty to remember that part.
> This will be repeated till every proposal was finished. They then retired to deliberate among themselves; and after deliberations were ended, the *sachem*, or some other councillor to whom he had delegated this office, replied to every part in its turn, with an exactness scarcely exceeded in the written correspondence of civilized powers. Each man actually remembered what was communicated particularly to him; and with this assistance the person who replied remembered the whole. (Beauchamp, p. 93.)

Morgan compared the evolution of the Iroquois tribal council to that of the Athenian senate, which had been in fact a council of chiefs, initiating measures which had to be submitted, in referendum, as it were, to the *ecclesia*, or assembly of the people, for acceptance or rejection. As the size of the body politic grew, the referendum became a separate institution by itself for special important projects.

With these stable democratic elements in place on the clan and tribal levels, "the formation of a confederacy became a question of intelligence and skill." (Morgan, p. 112.) Legend also would play a part, with a quasi-mythical heroic figure, Ha-yo-went'-ha, or Hiawatha, credited with being chief governor of that historic five-tribe council on Lake Onondaga. (Early writers assumed he was the same Hiawatha of Longfellow's celebrated poem, but it was later established that he was a Mohawk reformer and medicine man and no relation to Longfellow's hero based on Chippewa legend.)

Hiawatha's spokesman at the council was a wise man from the Onondaga, Da-ga-no-we'-da or Daganawida, who acted as interpreter and speaker to expound the structure and principles of the proposed confederacy. (Morgan, p. 113.) Other versions attribute to Daganawida himself the initiative for the move for intertribal unity and for converting Hiawatha from cannibalism to activism for "peace, civil authority, righteousness, and the great law." (See Hewitt; also *Encyclopedia Britannica, Micropedia*, vol. V, 1974, p. 432).

The confederacy was known indigenously as the *Ongwanonhsioni*, or "We of the Extended Lodge," or "We Longhouse Builders" after the long, wooden one-clan Iroquois homes.

1. The confederacy was a union of Five Tribes, composed of common *gentes*, under one government on the basis of equality; each Tribe remaining independent in all matters pertaining to local self-government.
2. It created a General Council of *Sachems*, who were limited in number, equal in rank and authority, and invested with supreme powers over all matters pertaining to the Confederacy.
3. Fifty *Sachems* were created and named in perpetuity in certain *gentes* of the several Tribes; with power in those *gentes* to fill vacancies as often as they occurred, by election among their respective members, and with the further power to depose from office for cause; but the right to invest those *Sachems* with office was reserved to the General Council.

Iroquois 97

4. The *Sachems* of the Confederacy were also *Sachems* in their respective Tribes, and with the Chiefs of these Tribes formed the Council of each, which was supreme over all matters pertaining to the Tribe exclusively.
5. Unanimity in the Council of the Confederacy was made essential to every public act.
6. In the General Council the *Sachems* voted by the Tribes, which gave to each Tribe a negative upon the others.
7. The Council of each Tribe had power to convene the General Council; but the latter had no power to convene itself.
8. The General Council was open to the orators of the people for discussion of public questions; but the Council alone decided.
9. The Confederacy had no Chief Executive Magistrate, or official head.
10. Experiencing the necessity for a General Military Commander they created the office in a dual form, that one might neutralize the other. The two principal Warchiefs created were made equal in powers.

(Morgan, p. 114.)

The framers of the U.S. Constitution may have found the Iroquois Confederacy a model to study and emulate. Morgan himself relates that "it is worthy of remembrance that the Iroquois commended to our forefathers a union of the colonies similar to their own as early as 1755," for "they saw in the common interests and common speech of the several colonies the elements of a confederation, which was as far as their vision was able to penetrate." (Morgan, p. 115.)

Certainly some of the features of the Onondaga agreement seem to find close duplication in the Philadelphia document. One of these is the electoral college, designed to give proper weight to the population of each state. Beauchamp draws the comparison:

> In voting by nations there was another feature. The *sachems* assigned to each nation were divided into classes, and in the national vote each class counted but one. The Mohawks, Oneidas, and Cayugas each had three classes of principal chiefs, the Senecas, four and the Onondagas, five. Thus, with the latter, it was not a majority of chiefs

but three classes at least that said what the Onondaga vote should be. It was much like our national electoral system. (Beauchamp, p. 424.)

The confederacy created the elective office of Hos-ga-a-geh-da-go-wa, "Great War Soldier," i.e., General Military Commander, in what was perhaps the first move ever to separate constitutionally military and civil power. In addition, two such commanders were chosen simultaneously, ensuring against "military takeovers." Furthermore, since war could only be declared by the council, military power, was, in effect, subjected to civilian control, a political innovation which was to become a crucial linchpin for successful modern democracies.

The five member tribes of the confederacy, joined later by the Tuscarora, retained their own self-government. Local autonomy was such a respected tradition that when the confederacy conquered other tribes, such as the Delawares, and held them in subjection, the subject tribes were allowed to remain under the government of their own chiefs, a colonial practice which latter-day British and American policy would attempt to meet halfway in Africa and Asia.

The Iroquois Confederacy, as a political instrument purely for external affairs of war and peace, "could not levy taxes, and it lacked a police force to carry out its decisions," Farb suggested, while conceding that "the League did somewhat resemble the union of the Thirteen Colonies in organization," that "it could more accurately be compared to the United Nations." (Farb, p. 98.)

As if to reinforce his own doubts about the democratic character of Iroquois society, Farb goes on to recall how "by a strange irony, the League of the Iroquois has become a model for Marxist theory." It seems that Friedrich Engels was fascinated by Morgan's book, *Ancient Society*, published in 1877, "at the very time that Karl Marx was working on the final volumes of *Das Kapital*." Engels passed on his enthusiasm to Marx, but Marx died before he could incorporate Morgan's theories in another book.

It was Engels who in 1884 was to write ecstatically of Morgan's depiction of the League of the Iroquois:

And a wonderful constitution it is... in all its childlike simplicity! No soldiers, no gendarmes or police, no nobles, kings regents, prefect, or judges, no prisons, no lawsuits... There cannot be any poor or needy—the communal household and the *gens* know their responsibilities towards the old, the sick, and those disabled in war. All are equal and free—the women included. (Friedrich Engels, *The Origin of the Family, Private Property, and the State.*)

Yet, at the worst, Marx and Engels appear to have been enthused by the success of the Iroquois in achieving that classless democracy for the achievement of which they were counseling the rest of the world first to accept a preliminary dictatorship of the proletariat. Farb thus succeeds in indicting not Iroquois democracy but the elusive promise of Marxism, with whose inevitably interminable repressive preliminaries the leaders in Peking are even now beginning to show signs of pragmatic weariness.

No internal dissension could kill the confederacy, and it enjoyed a solid, independent, democratic existence for more than two centuries until a powerful, disrupting external force, the American Revolution, rent it and scattered its tribes on both sides, the Mohawks and the Hurons with the British, the Oneidas and most of the Tuscaroras with the Americans. Ironically, a war that was to produce the democratic American republic put an end to a much earlier successful adventure into republican as well as direct democracy.

In their time the other great tribes of the North American continent would form their own leagues—the Creek Confederacy of six, the Ottawa Confederacy of three, the Dakota League of the "Seven Council-Fires," the Moqui Confederacy of Seven Pueblos, and the Aztec Confederacy in Mexico.

Each would display its own democratic creativity but none perhaps with as much lasting impact and, if you will, as much romance and panache as Minnie Thompson's redoubtable ancestors—the Iroquois.

14 The Tribes: Proving Jefferson Right

There are 283 federally recognized American Indian tribes in the United States. Before they were all finally subdued by the U.S. Army, the Iroquois, as we have just seen, stood tall on one end of the spectrum of political organization with their successful, cohesive, democratic confederacy. Of the tribes on the other extreme, some so devoid of central tribal organization that historians have been tempted to characterize them as totally anarchic, the most thoroughly researched and perhaps the most colorful appear to be the Navajos.

The Navajos are classified by anthropologists as an Athapascan people. Almost a millennium ago they came down from the north to the American Southwest, settling in their new homeland in what is now northeastern New Mexico, which they called Dinetah (their language is *dine bizaad*, of the Na-Dene family of languages). By the early 1600s they had migrated westward as far as the Black Mesa country of northern Arizona, and today this most numerous of all Indian tribes, with more than 400,000 members, occupies the largest reservation, straddling Utah, Arizona, and New Mexico.

I had heard of the unique achievement of this tribe—independence (until their defeat by the U.S. Army in 1864) with a minimum of political organization. To learn about how they did it, I traveled to Albuquerque in the summer of 1983 to talk to an eminent scholar on the Navajos, Dr. Robert W. Young, professor of anthropology at the University of New Mexico. Dr. Young has written extensively on Navajo political history. He tells of how the Navajos repeatedly baffled first the Spaniards and then the Anglo-Americans with their "loose sort of democracy, in which the rugged individualism and love for personal freedom, so long characteristic of the Navajos, were given the fullest possible latitude." For the white men, "it was an unorthodox system of government," conditioned as they were with their European culture "to coercive behavior and submission to authority as dominant features of their sociopolitical life." (Robert W. Young, *A Political History of the Navajo Tribe.* Tsaile, Ariz.: Navajo Community College Press, 1978.)

Yet, "loose as the internal control system was," the Navajos "maintained themselves as a dominant military power in the Spanish Southwest for more than two centuries, fending off conquest and retaining their independence while surrounded by enemies." (Young, pp. 31–32.)

By the time they were finally overrun by American numbers and firepower under the legendary Col. Christopher (Kit) Carson in 1864, the Navajos had not only "given mute testimony to the success of the tribal system" but proven that a lively democratic base with no coercive force above it can excel a centralized repressive system in providing the people not only with political stability but even with a lasting defensive military capability.

At the heart of the successful Navajo formula was "a social control system that respected the individual" in which "uniform collective behavior was achieved not by authoritarian directive imposed from above, but rather by creating a favorable public opinion within the local group." The favorable public opinion was obtained through a tedious but genuine democracy which sometimes required lengthy speeches and debate to reach unanimity. (Aubrey W. Williams, Jr., *Navajo Political Process.* Washington, D.C.: Smithsonian Institution Press, 1970, p. 7.)

With no centralized authority above them, the Navajo governed themselves "by the limits of acceptance of a culture, that is, a system of shared customs, beliefs, and values that was considered binding on the society." (Mary Shepardson, "Navajo Ways in Government," *American Anthropological Association*, vol. 65, no. 3, pt. 2, June, 1963, p. 46.)

In this the Navajos were merely continuing the consensual traditions of those cultures of Asia and the South Seas whence they are regarded to have originated. In Chapter 13 we saw Harland Cleveland's clarification that in those regions the passion for "unanimity, if possible" did not mean absolute unanimity, certainly not coerced consent. For the Navajos, "decisions," writes Shepardson, "should be unanimous if possible, should be 'talked over' with all interested adults, and should be executed voluntarily." Furthermore, "conformity should be secured through respect, praise, cooperation." (Shepardson, p. 48.) This applies to most decisions, from the election of leaders down to settlements of marital disputes, and is a process not unfamiliar to small, modern deliberative bodies, including juries and committees.

The most valuable application of this consensual process was in the choice of the local headman. At a later state in their independent life, the Navajos developed a system of dual leadership of peace and war chiefs for their local groups, enhancing further the uncoercive character of their society. The procedure for selecting both separately was identical, although the qualifications for each, of course, varied—the war leader noted for his ability to perform War Way chants; the peace chief for his "exemplary character, oratorical ability, personal magnetism, proven ability both in religious and practical affairs, and ability to perform the Blessing Way ceremony." (Williams, p. 6.)

At the election meeting to choose the local headman:

> while choice was nearly always unanimous, a close vote would prompt the people to request speeches from the various candidates. In addition, both men and women were allowed to speak in favor of a candidate. The speech-making and voting frequently took several days; a unanimous vote for one candidate was the objective, as great value was placed upon a community solidarity and harmony. (Williams, p. 6.)

Male and female equality was so pronounced that women were qualified to be elected even as war chiefs. (Williams, p. 6.) This should be revealing to Americans who are just now learning to accept, some with visible pain, the sight of feminine figures under those plumed shakos in West Point dress parades. All Navajo positions, in fact, were open "to the good man or the good woman." (Shepardson, p. 48.) As with some informal family dynasties in American politics, where the widow, the son or daughter, the brother or sister is apt to run for the seat of a departed politician, there was "a perceptible tendency" among the Navajos "for leadership to continue in the same family line." (Shephardson, p. 51.)

The status of the war chief appeared to be coequal with that of the *natani*, the civil headman, although apparently of shorter duration. The *natani* "remained a leader so long as his leadership enlisted public confidence or resulted in public benefit." (Young, p. 15.) However, there was at least a semblance of civilian supremacy over the military, with the war chief "supposed to obtain the consent of the *natani* before instituting a raid." (Shepardson, p. 53.) In any case, important "wars" could only be waged after approval by a war council attended by all adults.

On rare occasions requiring total tribal mobilization for peace or war, the Navajos managed to hold tribe-wide assemblies called *natc'ct* or *naach'id*. The last one on record was that held prior to the disastrous Navajo attack on Fort Defiance in 1858. It took four days of intense discussion to reach the decision to launch the attack. It is noteworthy that the chief medicine man for the assembly, a *natani* named Nataleeth ("known to the white men by the Mexican name of Sarcillas Largo"), openly dissented from the decision and walked out of the assembly apparently incurring no sanctions against himself. As we shall see, this tolerance to defiance in their society persists in modified forms among the Navajos of today.

Occasional full tribal councils did not mean permanent tribal government, and the baffling lack of a supreme Navajo authority led Spaniards like the Franciscan friar Alonso de Benavides to complain through emissaries of "so many captains among you." Unable to comprehend the workings of the native democracy, the Spaniards at various times themselves selected a "Paramount Chief of the Navajo Tribe." The artificial choice was "showered with gifts and symbols of authority." However, the Navajos never took them seriously and "rarely did the selected leader command the respect of more than three hundred to four hundred people." (Williams, p. 4.)

The Spaniards, and after them the Anglo-Americans, were driven to create these "instant" Navajo leaders after they realized that they had "labored under the delusion that the Headmen and War leaders were chiefs with coercive powers over the entire Tribe—political heads of state with whom binding treaties could be made and enforced." (Young, p. 30.) They desperately needed these treaties to keep the Indian tribes "pacified."

In the end it was not the treaties but the guns that subdued the Navajos. After the Carson victory, almost 10,000 Navajos were concentrated at Fort Sumner, "disorganized, facing disease and starvation." The U.S. Army began a series of experiments in synthetic Navajo governments, all of them, as Young puts it, "of the puppet variety," with the real authority in the hands of the military. A special Indian agent in Santa Fe, John Ward, rebelled against the practice of arbitrary selection:

> Making such a person the Chief of the Nation upon the mere saying of an officer... and without even the knowledge or consent of half of the Tribe, has always proved to be what it actually is, a perfect farce. No one Indian among them can be responsible, nor manage this tribe with any degree of success.... Besides, *their democratic notions of self-government are very strong.* (Young, p. 37. Italics in original.)

Today, it is not easy for an outsider to seek permission to attend councils of indigenous communities, whether in the United States or in Latin America. They are eager to guard their sacred traditions against alien encroachments. This very zeal for self-preservation is the guarantee that current community practices may indeed accurately reflect the substance, if no longer the exact forms, of their historical political democracy.

Sometimes scholars known for their objectivity gain admission to Indian councils. Williams is one of these, and he provides us with an insight into a contemporary Navajo council meeting. He notes that while the Navajos have adjusted to European-American models of political organization and have begun "to incorporate such political principles as majority rule, quorum, standing vote, and parliamentary procedures such as tabling a motion," nevertheless, "the meaning each of these political features has for Anglo-Americans is different from the meaning it has for the Navajo." (Williams, p. 53.)

For instance, Williams points out that "the presence of an active minority bloc of voters in a Navajo political meeting is viewed with considerable dissatisfaction and is thought to represent an unhealthy state of political affairs." (Williams, p. 53.) However, it is crucial to mark that while a minority bloc may cause dissatisfaction it is never punished for persisting in its minority position.

The traditional Navajo device for defusing the tensions caused by dissent is the "withdrawal." We saw this employed by Nataleeth, the chief medicine man in the 1858 *naach'id*, or tribal assembly, who after delivering his dissenting piece against the decision to make war, immediately "called for his horse and rode away." (Williams, p. 5.)

There are three ways identified by Williams by which the Navajos apply this technique today: nonattendance, having known of the agenda in advance; "doorway withdrawal," with individuals or groups standing at the door of the meeting hall where they can hear the discussion and can move either to the outside or inside to make a point or vote; or simply postponing consideration of the issue by the modern parliamentary "tabling" motion, in the hope that a future vote might produce a compromise proposal satisfactory to all.

Of the three modes, the doorway technique is the most creatively native to the Navajos. Williams offers some detail:

> At most chapter and grazing committee meetings one can observe clusters of men and women standing in the one or more doorways to the hall, even though there are available empty seats in the meeting hall. These clusters will reduce in size during the vote counting and passage in and out of the meeting hall is easiest during voting. During

the cold winter months the doorways to inside rooms such as the storerooms or kitchen of chapter houses are utilized by the "doorway" groups as strategic positions from which to withdraw or enter into activities of the group. (Williams, p. 56.)

To strict parliamentarians this may look like childish fence-sitting. However, if the exercise may be faulted for not encouraging clear lines of democratic dissent, it cannot be faulted for autocratic coercion. What the Navajos are displaying today is the same dislike for centralized repression and the same concern for harmony without sacrifice of individual opinion and dignity which their ancestors pursued and practiced.

A spot check of the rest of the 283 federally recognized American Indian tribes may reveal more conformity and less exceptions to this rule of democratic decision-making.

Among the Oglala Sioux in South Dakota, the councils of the chiefs and the warrior class, following traditions "running back for several centuries," arrive at decisions "through a continuous weighing of views until objections to the proposals have been reduced to a minimum." The wearisome process is justified by a "sensitivity for the feelings of the individual." A version of the Navajo "withdrawal" is available for dissenters who may "simply leave the group, thus evading the necessity for obeying a decision to which they were opposed." (Ira H. Grinnell, *The Tribal Government of the Oglala Sioux of Pine Ridge, South Dakota*. Special Project Number 22, Government Research Bureau, University of South Dakota, 1967, p. 13.)

In Alaska, among the Han Indians, "however despotic some chiefs might be," the popular will asserted itself in councils where "all the people of the community came together irrespective of age or sex in order to decide important questions and to elect chiefs." Even today among them "public opinion is very strong and each individual has great respect for the opinion of the community concerning his personal actions." (Cornelius Osgood, *The Han Indians*. New Haven: Yale University Department of Anthropology, 1971, p. 45.)

The democracy of the American Indian may mock the white man's claim to having transplanted the seeds of freedom in the New World from Europe. It also confirms, however, the eternal wisdom in Thomas Jefferson's declaration that all men are created equal. The Iroquois, the Navajos, the Sioux, the Hans—all knew they were created equal, and they lived in this conviction until new "undocumented aliens" came, troubling them with their doubts.

15 Aztecs: Mexican Schizophrenia

On July 15, 1867, the day of his triumphal reentry into Mexico City, Benito Juarez published a manifesto in which he proclaimed: "Between individuals as between nations, respect for the rights of others is peace." (See Charles Allen Smart, *Viva Juarez*. New York: J. P. Lippincott Company, 1963.)

In 1983, a Mexican consul in Washington, D.C., ironically also surnamed Juarez, refused me a visa to visit Mexico to research Aztec culture. I had presented a travel document issued to me by the U.S. Department of Justice as a refugee resident. The document had just been honored by the Sandinista Government of Nicaragua, by the Dominican Republic, Ecuador, Venezuela, and several Western European countries, but Consul Juarez rather rudely refused to honor it. Attempts by Mexican and American friends to intercede for me were in vain.

The inconsistency of the attitude of Consul Juarez with the solemn counsel by President Juarez on the rights of others appears to be in keeping with the schizophrenia with which Mexico conducts her domestic and foreign affairs. However, it is inspiring that respected Mexicans acknowledge this reality about themselves.

Shortly after my ill-fated visit to the Mexican consulate, the celebrated Mexican Carlos Fuentes would be telling his Harvard commencement audience that Mexico was "a modern, contradictory self-knowing and self-questioning nation." (Carlos Fuentes, Harvard Commencement Speech, June 9, 1983.) In December, 1984, President Miguel de la Madrid would allow a compatriot whom he had just decorated, Pablo Gonzalez Casanova, to tell him to his face that Mexico "curiously enough" understands the desire of the people for power "when it refers to what is new in Central America, but does not always seem to understand it with the same clarity when it refers to what is new in Mexico." (See Tom Wicker, "Getting the Message," The *New York Times*, December 23, 1984, op-ed page.)

A few months later, Peruvian novelist Mario Vargas Llosa, writing in the *Atlantic Monthly*, would direct a similar indictment for schizophrenic tendencies to West Germans, like the famous novelist Günter Grass. Grass, Vargas Llosa said, was guilty, along with many Western Europeans, of "an interesting double standard, an instructive schizophrenia," for advocating for developed countries democratic and representative institutions and for Latin America revolution and single-party government.

A single-party government like that of Mexico today, which was the target of that attack, in the presidential presence, by the awardee Gonzalez Casanova, was not part of the dream of Benito Juarez. When Juarez, the first full-blooded descendant of the Aztecs to rise to the presidency of modern Mexico, proclaimed the rights of all, "between individuals as between nations," he was seeking for Mexico the return of that indigenous pluralism which the Spaniards had suppressed in his society.

Jacques Soustelle, the French intellectual and scholar of Aztec history who broke with De Gaulle because the latter would not accept an independent Algeria within a pluralist French community, tells of the ideological clash between European absolutism and Mexican pluralism that resulted in the Spanish conquest of the Aztecs:

> For the Spaniards, for their part, were making "total" war; there was only one possible state for them, the monarchy of Charles V, and only one possible religion. The clash of arms was nothing to the clash of ideologies. The Mexicans were beaten because their thought, based upon a tradition of pluralism in both the political and the religious

aspects of life, was not adapted to contend with the dogmatism of the monolithic state and religion. (Jacques Soustelle, *Daily Life of the Aztecs*, Stanford: Stanford University Press, 1970, p. 214.)

While he was plotting his conquest of the Aztec, the conquistador began to analyze Aztec society using the parameters and nomenclature of his own Iberian monarchic culture. We have seen the same mistake committed by his counterparts who roamed Southeast Asia and fantasized a full-dress counterpart of feudal European society among the people of independent settlements in an archipelago which they would later baptize the Philippines, after the Spanish King Philip II.

So when the conquistador came upon Aztec military chiefs, he immediately equated them with nobles at the court of the king of Spain or of France. "But they were clearly mistaken," writes Soustelle, for these chiefs were not "hereditary magnates with great estates or inherited wealth" but "military or civil officials who enjoyed privileges that were attached to their office." The Aztec military, in contrast to the permanent hereditary European nobility, "continually renewed itself, taking recruits from the general body of the people; and this (as against the effeteness of some of the European nobility) was its great strength." (Soustelle, pp. 45–46.)

Mexican social historian Gonzalo Aguirre Beltran also marks the Spaniards' mistaken "preoccupation in giving leaders in the indigenous culture Castilian names, which conformed with modes of behavior with which they were familiar at the time, without considering that these names might have particular connotations and meaning fundamentally different from the phenomena which they were attempting to define." (Gonzalo Aguirre Beltran, *Formas de gobierno indigena*. Mexico: Inprenta Universitara, 1953, pp. 19–20, translation from Spanish mine.)

Aguirre Beltran and other authors assert that this carelessness with titles and functions led to the more grievous error of regarding the Aztec political reality as an authentic empire in the European sense of that term. Even a respected anthropologist like Elman R. Service refers to the "imperial success" of the Aztecs. (Elman R. Service, *Origins of the State and Civilization*. New York: Norton, 1975, p. 235.)

To fit this imperial mirage, Aguirre Beltran claims that "tribal councils were magically transformed to senates, the chiefs of the *caputlin* were converted to lords, the jurisdiction of the Indian tribes into kingdoms and chiefdoms." This imaginary political organization was "artificially patterned after a feudalism which was peculiar to a specific stage of the historical life of the West." (Aguirre Beltran, p. 45.)

Aguirre Beltran is joined by A.F. Bandelier, the renowned authority on American and Mexican Indian culture, in insisting that the Aztec "empire" was but a confederacy, "a partnership, formed for the purpose of carrying on the business of warfare, and intended not for the extension of territorial ownership, but only for an increase of the means of subsistence." (A. F. Bandelier, *On the Social Organization and Mode of Government of the Ancient Mexicans*. New York: Cooper Square, 1975, pp. 8–9.)

Aguirre Beltran likened the confederacy and its leaders to those of North American Indians of the nineteenth century, adding that Mexico, Texcoco, and Taclopan "were not capital cities of three kingdoms but, simply, the seats of three tribes whose *tecuhtlis* [chiefs] were not monarchs but only military leaders elected by a council of chiefs." (Aguirre Beltran, p. 20.)

Original Mexican society "rested on a democratic principle." (Bandelier, p. 3.) Avowing respect for Lewis Morgan's anthropological work on American Indians, Bandelier emulates Morgan's use of the *gens* or kinship group as focus for the study of indigenous Aztec political organization. He finds the Mexican *gens* ("kin") to be "a self-governing, therefore democratic cluster." Twenty such kins, with common territory, dialect, and worship, formed a tribe, which other authors, such as Victor Wolfgang von Hagen, would prefer to call a clan. (See Victor Wolfgang von Hagen, *The Ancient Sun Kingdoms of the Americas*. London: Panther, 1967). Von Hagen concedes that these clans were, at least "in theory democratic." Aguirre Beltran swears to the vigor of the original democracy and credits it with making inevitable the survival, even after Spanish domination, of such institutions as the tribal council and the election and recall of officials. (Aguirre Beltran, p. 27.)

The Aztecs called their tribal councils *Tlatocan*, or "place of speech," and the assembly house was known as *teepan*. Each *calpulli*, or territorial unit, was represented by a *tlatoani*, or "speaker," who was a man "of acknowledged ability and reputation." They met "possibly twice every Mexican month of twenty days," their meetings being "fully attended" and subject to be called "at any time."

The council performed both "directive" and "judicial" functions. Citing chronicler Friar Bernardino de Sahagun, Bandelier describes the due process accorded the accused in cases of theft or homicide:

> According to the rules of kinship, the *calpulli* was not only bound to avenge any wrongs suffered by one of its members, but it was also responsible for the offenses committed by the kinfolk towards any outsider. Hence theft committed outside of the *calpulli*, and especially the slaying, wilful or accidental, of members of one kin by those of another, became the cause of a claim by the offended *calpulli* upon that of the offender.
>
> This claim was submitted to the tribal council by the "speaker" of the complainant kinship. He produced his evidence, sometimes even in the shape of paintings, not so much to prove the facts as to sustain his claim. From the opposite side, the "speaker" defended the interests of his clan, and he also supported his pleadings with whatever testimony he might command. The remaining *"tlatoca"* [plural for *tlatoani*] listened attentively to both parties, and when the argument was concluded, they deliberated among themselves until they finally agreed upon an award. (Bandelier, pp. 95–97.)

Although there was no formal appellate body, reconsideration was possible before an "extraordinary gathering" which took place every eight days, attended by the council plus "the executive chieftains, the war-captains of the four great quarters, the 'elder brothers' of the kins, and the leading medicine men." (Bandelier, p. 87.)

There were also general assemblies of all the members of each *calpulli* reported by authors such as Alonzo de Zurita. It was convened to enable the chief to consult the people on serious problems, and writers such as José F. Ramirez are quoted as insisting that this "democratic element" predated the Spanish conquest. (Bandelier, pp. 79–80.)

The universal use of the electoral process on all levels of Aztec society should shake skeptics who have come to regard all non-European society as monolithic and despotic. It seems every official was elected, from the *tatloani* or "speaker" for the *calpulli*, the *tecuthli* (title applied to chiefs of provinces, "chief generals," judges of large towns, and even the head of the confederacy or, to use the controversial term, "emperor"), the separate peace and war chiefs, down to the four "war-captains."

The modern and, if you will, Anglo-Saxon notion that an elected official is not to be an absolute ruler but a "servant of the people" was apparently taught and propagated by the Aztecs. Mario Erdheim, of the University of Zurich, in a monograph published as part of a volume on the political economy and ideology of prehispanic Mexico, cites a passage from the *Codice Ramirez* (1878:35), which quotes some advice to Acamapichtli on his induction as *tatloani*:

> And so consider that you are not come to us for rest or recreation, but to assume new labors which are so weighty that they will keep you always at work, since you are the slave of this whole multitude which is now your lot to serve. (Mario Erdheim, "Transformaciones de la ideología Méxicana en realidad social," *Economía politica e ideología en el México prehispánico*. Mexico: Editorial Nueva Imagen, 1978, p. 207, translation from Spanish mine.)

"The nature of this [Aztec] government," writes Bandelier, "is expressed by the following rule of kinship, already found in vigor among northern [American] Indians: The kin had the right to elect its officers, as well as the right to remove or depose them for misbehavior." Sanguinely, he concludes that the *calpulli* was "consequently a DEMOCRATIC ORGANIZATION." (Bandelier, p. 79, emphasis Bandelier's.)

"The number of civil servants (*oficiales*) which this nation had for every little thing was great," records Soustelle. "There were clerks and minor officials (*mandocillos*) for everything, including the sweepers." (Soustelle, p. 41.) Also, if one were to interpret literally the following passage from Aguirre Beltran, all these civil servants were elected!

> The Indian chiefs (*indios cabezas*), meeting in council, elected the functionaries of the *calpulli* who were charged with carrying out their decisions. Of these functionaries the most prominent was the *teachcauh*, the senior elder (*pariente mayor*), [who] was in charge of the communal administration of the *calpulli*, its agricultural production, the work of its men, order, justice and worship of its gods and ancestors. He was the advocate and representative of the kin before the tribal government and as such was a member of the tribal council.
> Of equal importance as a functionary was the *tecuthli*, the lord as he is translated by chroniclers, or the grandfather according to Bandelier, [who] was the military chief of the *calpulli*....
> Other important functionaries of the *calpulli* were the *tequitlatos*, in charge of communal labor; *calpizques*, tribute collectors, *tlayacanques*, bowmen (*cuardrilleros*), the priests and medicine men in whose care was entrusted the psychological welfare of the group; and a number of minor civil servants at the head of whom were the *topiles* who performed police functions. We should not forget in this enumeration the *tlacuilo*, clerk, or better, painter of hieroglyphics, who was the historian of the *calpulli*....
> The functionaries of the *calpulli* remained in office for life; furthermore, since they were elected their children and descendants did not inherit their office, and they could, for grave cause, be deposed at the will of the council. The functionaries of the *calpulli*, besides, were always elected among the Indian chiefs, among the heads of families or elders of the clan. It may be assumed that only the *topiles* (*to*, our, *pilli*, son) were not elected among these venerable members of the kin. (Aguirre Beltran, pp. 22–24.)

Soustelle calls the *calpulli* chief executive the *calpullec* and, unlike Aguirre Beltran who is careful to define the limitations of the Aztec electorate, says simply that he "was elected to his office by his fellow citizens."

It is not until the rise of the tripartite confederacy among the Nahuatl tribes of Mexico, Tezenco, and Tlacopan that we begin to hear of an Aztec "emperor." His indigenous title was *tlacatecuthli*, or "chief of men." Since he was elected and could be deposed, a more appropriate modern term for him might be (as Minoo Masani suggests for the Indian Buddhist *raja* of the sixth century, B.C.) president of the republic. The *Codex Mendoza* records that the first incumbent of this office was "elected by popular vote" in the year 1375. "From that time on the office remained strictly elective and non-hereditary." (Bandelier, p. 114.) However, the incumbent could be deposed "for misdemeanor," and during the period of the conquest, the last Montezuma, known as "Wrathy Chief, the younger," was removed from office. Before he met his violent death his successor was duly elected. (Bandelier, p. 118.) The Spaniards imposed a sort of caste system on the Aztecs, "cataloguing them like children subject to guardianship which became the pretext for iniquitous exploitation." (Aguirre Beltran, p. 48.) Even before the conquest, however, some stratification already had taken place in Aztec society, distinguishing the *piles*, or aristocracy, from the *macehuales*, or working class. (Aguirre Beltran, p. 48.) Furthermore, as the city and the confederacy grew larger, the body that elected the sovereign grew smaller. By the beginning of the sixteenth century, only about a hundred persons formed the electoral college—*tecuthlatoque*, supreme dignitaries; *achcacauhtin*, second-rank district officials; and *tlenamacazque*, the more important priests. A small oligarchy was now running the affairs of state. "The change was very great," writes Soustelle, "and it had come about in a very short time: tribal democracy had been replaced by an aristocratic and imperialistic monarchy." (Soustelle, p. 37.)

Yet, transformation at the top, even later, at the hands of the Spaniards, would not kill the original democracy. In the process of acculturation that took place after the disorganization of the indigenous culture by the conquest, two diametrically opposed "tendencies" emerged—one leading to feudalism, the other, of greater force and consistency, toward democracy. (Aguirre Beltran, p. 28.)

The original democratic electoral process did not guarantee that the Aztec laws and customs executed by the elected officials were themselves consistent with twentieth-century standards of constitutional democracy. Not all medieval Western laws, in fact, can thus measure up. There were also obviously brutal practices, such as human sacrifice, which annoyingly persist in one's impression of Aztec culture. It is, of course, small consolation to recall that other races, like that of the Druids in England, once also practiced it and for perhaps lesser reasons. For the Aztecs, the victim, usually one captured in war, "was no longer an enemy who was to be killed but a messenger, arrayed in dignity that was almost divine, who was sent to the gods." (Soustelle, p. 99.) For the Celtic Druids, although "there is very little indication... that human sacrifice was widespread and frequent practice" among them, it was not unheard of "to offer the first born of their children to the great stone idol, Mag Slecht." (T. D. Kendrick, *The Druids*. London: Methune & Co., 1921, p. 17.)

In any case, perhaps less civilized killings were indulged in by the invading Spaniards who "so sincerely moved by the cruelty of the native priests, nevertheless massacred, burnt, mutilated and tortured with a perfectly clear conscience." (Soustelle, p. 99.)

The nobler legacy of the Aztecs would surface stubbornly and repeatedly throughout modern Mexican history. The career of Benito Juarez was only one, although perhaps the most memorable one, of these surfacings. Someday the schizophrenia will be overcome, and Mexico will stand, no longer, as Carlos Fuentes puts it, "contradictory self-knowing and self-questioning," but tall and self-confident among the certified democratic nations of the world.

16 Incan Empire: The Democratic Fringe

The autocratic track of the dual tendency in Mexican society, produced by Spanish "aristocratization" of the original elective Aztec leaders was broadened even more by the Mayan heritage from the Mexican Southwest, which did not share the multi-level electoral and consensual habits of the Aztecs.

The Mayan ruler, the *halach uinic*, wielded absolute powers, "restrained only by a council who were presumably related to him by blood ties." (Victor Wolfgang von Hagen, *The Ancient Sun Kingdoms of the Americas*. London: Panther, 1967, p. 165.) His office was hereditary, and only if no surviving sons or, in their default, brothers were available for succession did the council step in to choose a successor, "probably a relative of the late lord with the same patronymic." (von Hagen, p. 166.)

There was also a rigid four-class stratification: the nobility (*Ahau*), the most powerful clan, enjoying exclusive privileges along with the chiefs of other "collaborator" clans; the tributaries, or the industrial and agricultural class; the slaves, mostly war captives; and the priesthood, with considerable influence on the monarch. A subclass of the priesthood with particularly nauseous duties was the *nacon*, a sort of executioner who was charged with slitting open victims' chests to extract their hearts in human sacrifice. (See Juan de D. Perez Galaz, *Derecho y organización social de los Mayas*. Mexico: Gobierno Constitucional del Estado de Campeche, 1943.)

The Mayans produced immortal art and architecture, but, unlike their Aztec neighbors, they left little to contribute to the Mexican heritage of popular participation. Southward across the Andes, the other great civilization of pre-Columbian Latin America, the Incas, was an even poorer source for democratic tradition.

Unlike Louis XIV, the "Sun King of France" who had specifically insisted that he was the state, the Sun King of Peru, Sapa Inca, never had to bother to make the claim. Everyone in his realm conceded that everything belonged to him—the land, the earth, the people, the gold ("the sweat of the sun"), and the silver ("the tears of the moon"). (von Hagen, p. 269.)

Even that other descendant of the sun across the ocean, the Mikado of Japan, had to confront shoguns and warlords who successfully circumscribed his power. Only the priests exercised limited powers independent of the Inca emperor.

Yet the almighty, expanded Inca empire was relatively short-lived. Its conquest of neighboring ethnic groups commenced in the early fifteenth century. Barely a hundred years later, the Spaniards would land, kidnap the emperor Atahuallpa, and, after a series of deceptive tactical moves, split the empire and finally destroy it.

Within those years the Incas extended their rule, the imperial Tawantinsuyu, to more than 12 million people who spoke at least twenty unrelated languages, recruiting one ethnic group to garrison another, resettling loyal populations in hostile or newly conquered territories, and otherwise successfully employing fear to keep their subject nations under control. (See "Inca Political Structure," *Proceedings of the 1958 Annual Spring Meeting of the American Ethnological Society*, pp. 30–41.)

However, the Andean terrain was always a challenge to day-to-day government, and the absolutism of the Incas would not succeed in smothering the "cake of custom" of more distant nations. In November, 1982, I visited with three such nations in Ecuador—the Saraguros, the Otavalos, and the Shuaras.

The Saraguros inhabit the region adjacent to the city of Loja, which has become a center for regional development in southern Ecuador, at the border of Peru. They speak Quichua, the language once used officially by the Inca empire. (Today news broadcasts in southern Ecuador are done both in Quichua and Spanish.) They are fiercely independent, and the Ecuadorian government respects the sacredness of their institutions, including the secrecy of the meetings of their council, which may not be attended by government representatives. Once a pre-Spanish conquest body, the council is now affiliated with the Federación Inter-Provincial de Indigenas Saraguros.

When I asked, anyway, if I could be admitted to a council meeting, Victor Vacacela, the chief of the community of 300 families outside of Loja, firmly said no. He also demanded to know, before answering any more of my questions, if I was a spy. "You mean of the Americans?" I said with an innocent smile. "Of course not," he replied, looking at me straight in the eye. "I mean of the Ecuadorian government in Quito!"

Over draughts of *machanayaco* (fermented sugar cane juice) Vacacela grew more mellow and loquacious. The Saraguros, he said diffidently, were a "humble, pure race" transplanted by the Incas from Bolivia because they were thought to be "assimilable." Recalling my readings of Inca imperial strategy, I thought the reason for the forced migration might have been the opposite—that the Incas had found them intransigent where they were and decided to move them away to keep them from infecting the other conquered nations with their resistance.

Vacacela was born in that community and had been its chosen leader for twenty years. He described how the community council (*tandanacuy runacon*), summoned to meetings with a *quipa*, a native brass horn, held dialogues (*parlanacuna tocuy* or originally *rimanacuy*) for every important decision, including the election of officers, such as the chief (*tukoy runakunata pusha*, also called in Spanish *alcalde mayoral*).

Vacacela complained of discrimination against Saraguros in government schools where children "wearing only rubber shoes" were sent out of the classrooms. He said the religious schools run by the Spanish Escolapio fathers did not indulge in such petty unfairness.

Up the hill from Vacacela's community I talked to Escolapio Father Antonio Alonso, from Santander, Spain, parish priest of another community of 600 Saraguro families. He told me of the free discussions in the community councils where the elders (*tantanirata rurah*), who still retain the traditional values of their race, are now getting inhibited in discussions in front of younger, more educated members. Nevertheless, it is the "best speaker" that dominates the debate which is presided over by the *tukoy runakunata pusha*.

There was no repressive element in the indigenous culture, Father Alonso asserted. The Saraguros are by nature "soft" (Spanish *suave*) compared to the "rough Europeans." Punishment for offenses against customary laws consisted mostly of "isolation," a sanction reminiscent of the "ostracism" in the South Seas culture from which the Saraguros may have ultimately originated.

A converse reputation is enjoyed by the Shuaras, "the only autochthonous American group that successfully resisted the Spanish empire." (Michael J. Harner, *Shuar, Land of the Sacred Cascades*. Quito: Ediciones "Mundo Shuar," 1978, p. 1.) I talked to young Shuaras who have opened a documentation center in Quito (the Mundo Shuar, Centro de Documentación, Investigación y Publicaciónes), in their determined drive to overcome negative generalizations about their race, stemming mostly from their head-hunting traditions. They insisted that free consensus was also a practice in their society.

However, the contrary evidence from credible writers is difficult to ignore. Hernan Gallardo Moscoso, writer and former provincial registrar, told me in Loja of strict authoritarian family rules whereby the husband in a Shuar family may even forbid his wife to speak Spanish. The Shuar chiefs were hereditary, but their authority was important only in times of war. There is no formal political or tribal organization even today.

There are about 40,000 Shuars at present, speaking a language distinct from the more universal Quichua. For a time they were under heavy missionary activity, but the Ecuadorian government has restored much of their autonomy, and they are left to govern themselves under their own customary law. They apply penalties for offenses by means of informal guerrilla action by offended parties and their relatives who are entitled to carry out strict revenge based on a principle not far removed for the Hebraic "eye for an eye." Thus, the sanction for homicide is counterhomicide. (Harner, pp. 159–60.) Gallardo Moscoso, however, spoke of an occasional Shuar dialogue of strong words, which results in eventual mutual understanding among the parties.

Two-hours drive north of Quito is the base of the community of the Otavalos, a much more open, Quichua-speaking indigenous people. They have been compared to gypsies because of their success as traveling singers and merchants, wandering as far as Spain and other parts of Western Europe.

I was introduced to Luis German Perugachi, secretary of the community government, who told me that in earlier days his office would have borne the title *quillcac camayu*. The chief was called *curaca*, and his office was "sometimes hereditary." One of his more important duties was to preside over the general assembly, the *jatun tandanacuy*, which was attended by all the community. The assembly was convened with a calling horn similar to the *quipa* of the Saraguros or by *capari* (Spanish *griterio*), "shouting from high places."

At the assembly meeting anyone with a problem was entitled to speak up. Consensus on a solution was reached by prolonged discussion.

This popular consensual process persists to this day and is used to solve such mundane questions as changing of dress from traditional to modern. The Otavalo dress code is extremely strict, and it takes an assembly decision to permit an individual to shed his colorful poncho cape and stiff black hat for a sweater, jeans, and baseball cap. The hirsute code is even stricter and theoretically allows no exception even with assembly permission. All Otavalo men wear pigtails, even today. Perugachi told me of a movement in the 1950s among young members of the community to allow wholesale modernization of hairstyles. It was quickly quashed by community consensus.

In the old days violations of Otavalo customary laws interpreted in assembly decisions were sanctioned by corporal punishment, *charinimin* or *charachuasca* (Spanish *azote de cuerpo*, body lashing), or by *naricunaya*, or boycott or ostracism, a penalty which seems to be prevalent in Andean cultures. Antonio

Gramal, the head of the community, remembered instances of *naricunaya* being applied to Otavalos who insisted on adopting modern dress in spite of negative assembly decisions. As elsewhere, notably the South Seas, ostracism may be viewed as democratic or intolerantly autocratic depending on from which side the view is taken. As a mild form of dealing with deviants, it could be regarded as reflective of a tendency in the society to be lenient toward dissent. On the other hand, that the dissenter is punished at all does not speak well of the community's sense of tolerance, which is a valuable element in democratic society. Doubts about how to categorize the political character of the society might be resolved, however, by the crucial fact that the sanction is administered by a decision arrived at by community consensus and not by a despotic chief.

While they are proud to have preserved their original consensual culture throughout Inca and Spanish domination, the Otavalos are also proud to recount that they stood fast by Atahuallpa when he was kidnaped by the Spaniards, until his death, contrasting themselves with other races who rushed to the Spanish side in order to rid themselves of Inca tyranny. In that pragmatic stance, these other races were presaging twentieth-century Western colonies like Indonesia, which availed themselves of the invading Japanese to attain independence from the European master.

Certainly, unlike the Shuaras, the Otavalos are not conscious of any pressure to correct popular impressions of their culture. They maintain, with the aid and encouragement of the Ecuadorian government, their own cultural research center, the Instituto Otavaleno de Antropologia, much more elaborate and impressive than the spunky documentation center of the young Shuaras in Quito, undertaking research and producing material of much self-confidence and positiveness.

The Aztecs, Mayans, and Incas, along, in microcosm, with the Saraguros, Shuaras, and Otavalos, appear to confirm the coexistence of autocratic and democratic strands in the weave of original societies, as well as the more striking resilience of the fiber of indigenous democracy.

17 Bantu Assembly: Original South African Democracy

In November, 1884, fourteen Western nations sat down in Berlin for a three-month conference during which they proceeded to "carve up Africa like a Christmas turkey."

A decade earlier, after having "nibbled at the edges of the continent for several centuries," the Europeans had begun a mad rush into the interior, laying claim "to more than ten million square miles of territory and one hundred million people in the space of a decade." (Glenn Frankel, "How Europeans Sliced Up Africa." The *Washington Post*, January 6, 1985, op-ed page.)

The indiscriminate dismemberment of what were once several hundred independent states resulted in the fragmentation of tribes and their regrouping into artificial populations with peoples of radically different cultures and religions. This engendered intramural rivalries that triggered prolonged wars such as that between the Ibo and Hausa in formerly British-ruled Nigeria.

After the settling of the imperialist dust and the subsequent liberation, there emerged an Africa of newly independent states searching for ways to rationalize national identities out of the spurious territorial divisions that were the legacy of the European masters.

In South Africa, the problem of the black African was compounded by a unique phenomenon in the European penetration of the continent—white settlers had come in numbers two centuries before the Berlin Conference of 1884–1885 who would strike deep roots in the velds and escarpments and later, although comprising only 17 percent of the population, steadfastly refuse to give up repressive political control of the republic.

The descendants of the Dutch, French, and German settlers, who speak Afrikaans, a corruption of the Dutch tongue, and who comprise 60 percent of the white population, and the English-speaking 40 percent, would find in the humor of "The Flintstones" the faithful reenactment of the sophistry in their treatment of the Bantu, who compose fully 70 percent of the country's total population.

The Flintstone family is lovable but laughable because "everyone knows" that primitive people like them could in no way have behaved as civilly and democratically as they do. So also do the South African whites regard the Bantu blacks as worthy of patronizing affection but not of democratic rights; for these rights are, as we have already seen Americans such as William F. Buckley, Jr., insist, a subtle "metaphysical patrimony" which the Bantu cannot yet understand. So the Bantu must be regarded as part of that "three quarters of the world" which, we have also seen another American hold, "are not culturally adapted to democracy."

It is, of course, difficult to predict just when the Bantu can be expected to become culturally adapted to appreciate this metaphysical patrimony since, as black Africans, they are to be regarded, in the Darwinian scheme of natural selection, as among the most recent dismounters from the proverbial simian tree—all this in spite of the accumulating evidence that the first man in fact appeared (or, to pacify the Darwinians, evolved) in Africa.

The lyricist's sermon, sung by the historical character of the Rev. Josiah Strong, Congregationalist minister in Cincinnati, justifying the American seizure of the Philippines in 1898, might well be intoned by a South African prime minister today:

> And now we come to those ideas of the Anglo-Saxon,
> Those two which led our race relentlessly to wax on:

Namely, civil liberty that gives men true equality
And Christianity less Romanish frivolity!

This in fact's the scientific and astute opinion
Of him who authored all those brilliant theories Darwinian.

We are the perfect products of a natural selection,
For in our veins superior traits have entered by injection!

(Raul S. Manglapus, *Philippines: Silenced Democracy.* New York: Orbis Books, 1976, p. 101.)

The Reverend Strong's notions are desperately clung to by only a few American extremists today. In the United States blacks may still have a good fight for equality ahead of them, but they are now governing in many cities even where they are not in the majority. In South Africa, the black majority may not vote.

The Bantu majority is really made up of four main ethnic groups: the Nguni, including the Xosa, Swazi, Zulu, and Ndebete; the Sotho, comprising the Tswanda, Pedi, and Sotho proper; the Venda; and the Thonga. There also exist the Khoisan peoples—Bushmen and Hottentots. Before the white man came, some of these tribes had already been voting in their popular assemblies. Some chiefs traditionally assumed office by formal election, although other methods of rising to office were possible, such as birthright, "use of wealth," or military achievement. (Isaac Schapera, *Government and Politics in Tribal Societies.* London, Watts, 1956, p. 50.)

Among the Zulu, the king, in carrying out his duty to maintain the customary law, was expected to follow the advice of his council, which was made up of chiefs and close advisers. It was not an idle expectation. If he did not follow the conciliar advice, he suffered the indignity of having one of his cattle taken away from him by the council. (See M. Fortes and E. E. Evans-Pritchard, *African Political Systems.* London: Oxford University Press, 1940.) During the council meetings, the agenda and order of speakers were arranged so that the councillors would not appear to be defying the king, who was, nevertheless, morally bound to respect the will of the majority. Fortes

128 Will of the People

and Evans-Pritchard describe the peculiar protocol which was applicable even to lower-level tribal councils:

> In council the king (or a chief) was supposed to put the matter under discussion before the council and himself speak last so that no one would be afraid to express his own opinion. The king might inform his close councillors of his views and they could put these to the council; he should not put himself in a position where he would be contradicted. But no councillor should express a strong opinion; he should introduce his points with some oblique phrase deferring to the king. The king ended the discussion and, if he were wise, adopted the views of the majority. The council could also initiate discussions on matters of tribal or national interest. It seems that in fact the king did consider his councillors' views and did not act autocratically. (Fortes and Evans-Pritchard, p. 33.)

In the king's council there were, besides the chiefs, the *indunas*, men of debating skill and ability, the two most important of whom were the commander of the army and the prime minister (great *induna*). Lesser *indunas* were in charge of wards at which level "all the people were entitled to express their opinion on affairs," doing this "through the heads of their kinship groups and their immediate political officers." (Fortes and Evans-Pritchard, p. 39.)

Aside from his "confidential advisers" (the *bagakolodi*), the identity of some of whom may not be known to the public, a Bantu chief "also has a formal and much wider council, which meets as a body to discuss important questions of public policy." (Schapera, pp. 42–43; see also Robert F. Stevenson, *Population and Political Systems in Tropical Africa*. New York: Columbia University Press, 1968.) Some of its members, who include all subchiefs, prominent headmen, and influential persons, live permanently at the capital. The meetings, held about once a year, are always public, open to anybody else who wishes to come. The exceptions are the councils of the Tswana and the Venda, which are strictly private, and nobody may attend unless personally invited, paralleling the secrecy that we have observed of tribal meetings in South Seas, Asian, and indigenous American cultures.

The council is the tribe's main deliberative assembly, except among the Sotho, and its decisions are binding on all members of the tribe. Among the Sotho, especially the Tswana, there is a special type of popular assembly commonly called *pitso*, which meets almost weekly and which all tribesmen are expected to attend—on some occasions on a compulsory basis, such as meetings to pass new laws.

The *pitso* arrives at a decision through the tedious consensual process also developed in other societies in other continents, but the ideal of unanimity does not exclude recognition of minority views. "If the discussion reveals marked disagreement, the chief may ask the men to group themselves according to their views, and the relative strength of the different parties is then clearly seen." (Schapera, p. 44.)

The frequency of tribal meetings varies according to the local pattern of settlement which sometimes makes arrangements for convening difficult. However, the general rule of free discussion and respect for dissent appears to brook no exception.

In the following transcript of the minutes of a meeting in Kgatla of a Tswana tribe, held in May, 1924, we note a variation of the consensus process—an actual vote by raising of hands:

Segale Pilane (chief's uncle and principal adviser): We seek a plan for dealing with beer-drinking. Beer has ruined us; we have no children; we tried to educate them, but beer has spoiled them....

Abel Madia: Let the sale of beer be prohibited. [Supported by seven others.]

Chief Isang: I endorse the suggestion that beer should no longer be sold. But now I ask, is there not some one who can suggest a law whereby beer may continue to be sold, but in such a way as not to cause trouble among the people?

Maretele Mangole: Let beer be sold, but the purchaser should go home to drink it.

Pule Mogomotsi: Let it be sold, but on condition that it is no longer drunk at night.

Mothswane Pilane: Let beer-drinking at night be prohibited, and also let beer be sold only for consumption at home.

Kgari Pilane: Beer-drinking goes together with sexual immorality. You should not find fault with the boys alone, and ignore the girls. As long as beer continues to be brewed, immorality will be associated with it.

Mabuse Letsebe: I say, let beer continue to be sold....

Chief Isang: Let those who say that beer should not be sold raise their hands.

(Eighty-five raised their hands; only two said that beer should still be sold.)

Chief Isang: You are not of two opinions, you are unanimous. And what I say to you is that when you go astray and are turned back you should listen. To err is human, but to find fault with oneself is often lacking. Therefore I say: Beer must no longer be drunk at night. See to it that beer is brewed not by the girls but by their mothers. I shall allow the brewing and sale of beer from the beginning of June until December, and if there is no improvement I shall call you together again to kill the sale of beer. (Schapera, pp. 141–42.)

Chief Isang appears to ignore the two dissenters in announcing: "You are unanimous." Of course, eighty-five out of eighty-seven is near unanimity, and the relevant point is that all were free to voice their opinion, and there were no ill consequences to dissent. In the end, the chief decided on a middle course, which was an obvious attempt to reconcile the eighty-five with the two, demonstrating concern for the position of the diminutive minority. Most important of all, there had been open and unfettered consultation before the chief took action, a universal character of tribal government among all Bantus.

In fact, although most Bantu chiefs hold hereditary positions, they are "helpless when faced by collective resistance to his commands." Among the Hottentots, both the Schapera and Fortes/Evans-Pritchard studies stress, the chief is only primus inter pares within the council. Everywhere among the Bantus, the authority of the chief is so circumscribed by the council and popular opinion that he has often had to drop a policy in the face of broad opposition. "The king is ruled by his councillors," say the Swazi, and a stubborn king "in olden days would run severe risk of dying by poisoning." (Schapera, p. 145.)

The universal rule of consultation is applied with uneven frequency depending on the size and disposition of the tribal population. The smaller groups, like the Bergdama and the Bushmen, gather daily around the campfire. In bigger ones, notably among the Tswana, popular assemblies on the national level have to be held fairly often.

In the Bantu system, however, there is no perfect equality in the availability of major posts in the central government. Only "nobles" (*dikgosana*) and "commoners" (*badintlha* or *batlhanka*) may apply. (Stevenson, p. 77.) However, on the local tribal level all classes are qualified, and, as we have noted, popular assemblies are open to all (except, Fortes and Evans-Pritchard note, the serfs among Western Tswana).

The bottom line in the character of South African tribal government, however, is the political interdependence between the chief and his people. No matter how he rises to office "a chief is chief by grace of his people" and "rarely has any chief been able to rule oppressively for long." The indigenous system has within it the checks and balances required for nonarbitrary rule, and even "if not democratic in the sense of being able to elect their rulers, South African communities can at least often restrain them and if sufficiently provoked get rid of them." (Fortes and Evans-Pritchard, p. 211.)

In an ironic way, the political isolation of the South African blacks today has helped to preserve their original indigenous democracy. They were democratic before the white man arrived. Today, Desmond Tutu is correct in demanding to know why this original democracy is not integrated into the republic.

18 One-Party System: Un-African Activity

In October, 1984, I traveled to Kampala, the capital of Uganda, to attend a meeting of the Christian Democratic International (CDI), the world organization of political parties of Christian Democratic orientation. The Democratic Party of Uganda, now the major opposition group, is an affiliate, and its president, Paul Ssemogerere, is a vice-president of the CDI.

With its adherence to the CDI and Christian Democratic ideology, a nonconfessional political creed, the Democratic Party has provided itself with an international base from which to launch a peaceful but sweeping change in Ugandan politics—the transformation of parties from tribal political machines to nationally based organizations advocating transnational democratic philosophies. It is not a painless mission. The politics of Uganda, like that of all former European colonies in Africa, is enmeshed in tribal animosities mostly sharpened by the artificial carving up of the continent at the Berlin Conference of 1884–1885.

Uganda is a particularly explosive case. It is made up of former long-standing kingdoms and tribal states, including the kingdoms of Buganda and Bunyoro, rearranged by the British, including what is now Kenya, as the colony of British East Africa. At the time of my visit, the president of the republic was Milton Obote. He is of the Lango tribe, in the Northern Lira District, while Ssemogerere is an Mpigi, from the former kingdom of Buganda, where Kampala is located. The strength of Ssemogerere's Democratic Party is among the population of Buganda.

After the murderous Idi Amin regime, the current Ugandan effort at political pluralism is valiant and correct. It is not yet a success. Obote's regime is not in full control of the army, which has been accused of rampaging abuses in the countryside. However, the effort appears to be more in keeping with indigenous African tribal politics than the one-party system to which many African leaders have resorted, using the very tensions between African tribes as their excuse. (In 1985, Obote was deposed in still another coup.)

Ethiopian anthropologist Asmarom Legesse, professor at Swarthmore College, believes that the African advocates of the one-party state are "quite mistaken" in not appreciating "the value of an adversary relationship in African political life." In an interview at Swarthmore in 1983, he told me of his admiration for Julius Nyerere of Tanzania (the man responsible for helping depose Amin in neighboring Uganda) "who makes a concerted effort to link the political institutions of his country to the African cultural foundations and has done more than any other African leader to combat the dangers of political alienation." He praised the Tanzanian leader for believing "that political culture should not be imposed from without, but should grow organically out of the historic and cultural roots."

Yet, Legesse felt that Nyerere has been wrong in his "assessment of the character of traditional African political culture," opting for the one-party state and ignoring the important reality of conflict and pluralism in both egalitarian and hierarchical African societies.

In egalitarian African systems Legesse has found that "political groups are often balanced in such a way that the groups alternate in acceding to power or they hold slightly differentiated forms of authority which are counterpoised." Thus, spheres of authority overlap, making mutual regulation possible. In Eastern Africa, where societies are graded by age-sets, there are generational groups that balance each other. For instance, it may be surprising to note that "father and son usually fall into opposite camps," thus transforming "an inherently authoritarian relationship into one of egalitarian dialogue and institutionalized mutual regulation." Legesse asserted that this was true not only at the level of the family but at the level of the political system as a whole.

What is perhaps more surprising and, indeed, fascinating is the manner in which checks and balances are built into the hierarchical, or monarchic, African systems. One institution countervailing the power of the king was the office of the queen mother who "often had her own palace and distinct court." Her role was to counsel the king, particularly if he was still an adolescent. At other times, she "headed a court of appeal to which citizens could take their case if the decision of the king proved to be unjust."

Legesse confirmed the role of the "council of king makers" who chose the successor upon the death of a king. He said that in Buganda, the councillors were organized into a formal parliament known as the *Lukiko*, "which exercised considerable legislative and juridical authority." He concluded with a direct indictment of the African one-party systems: "There is no doubt that conflict, in its institutionalized form, is the cornerstone of African systems of distributive justice. It is, therefore, a mistake for African political leaders to believe that institutionalized political conflict is alien to African political morality."

Legesse is perhaps best known in anthropological literature for his work *Gada: Three Approaches to the Study of African Society*, in which he analyzes the heavily ritualistic but, nevertheless, authentic pluralism among the Borana, most of whom live in his native Ethiopia and whose traditions have been preserved unchanged for centuries. He spent many years researching the rites passage of Borana from age-set to age-set and following the election of councillors at each level. The Gada is "a system of classes (*luba*) that succeed each other every eight years in assuming military, economic, political and ritual responsibilities." (Asmaron Legesse, *Gada: Three Approaches to the Study of African Society*. New York: Free Press, 1973, p. 87.)

In the summer of 1963 he observed the election of *adula* (senior) councillors. A strict democratic code required that the clan hold a general meeting (*cora*) every eight years to elect six men who would compose the council of electors. These councils were now about to hold public electoral assemblies. Legesse describes the lively public interest in the event:

For about two months Borana was much more agitated than it is under normal circumstances. Everywhere I went, I saw men huddled together near marketplaces, around wells, and near settlements arguing about the approaching proclamation ceremony (*lallaba*). As I traveled from Negelli to Moyyale to Arero along an approximately triangular course over the eastern half of Boranaland, I was astonished to find a remarkably high level of interest in the events. (Legesse, p. 205.)

Legesse decided to concentrate on the elections among the Gona moiety since it had fourteen clans, and there was "therefore an acute rivalry between clans to get at least one man to represent them in the *adula* council," which allowed only three members per clan. All moieties must be equally represented in the council and, Legesse writes, "so far as we can tell, there have been no exceptions to this rule in the past century." All the candidates were free to speak and were, as well, liable to be subjected to public criticism at the assembly. Legesse saw one candidate chastised for "failure to resist invaders and for the inefficacy of his rainmaking ritual." Despite Borana tradition that would normally disqualify the candidates because of these "shortcomings," the council of electors chose to overlook them "because of his personal qualities and his overall success as a *gada* leader." Another candidate impressed Legesse with his "defiant oratory and his powerful speaking voice," which seemed to fulfill Borana expectations of *dubbi* (eloquence)— not unlike in Western elections "the sine qua non of leadership." Anglo-Saxon diffidence is not without its parallel in the Borana culture, which "tolerates self-adulation when the speaker is comparing himself with his political rivals, but also demands humility when the speaker sees himself in confrontation with Borana as a whole." A candidate who does not find enough support in his moiety has the alternative of turning to his age-mates and, if this fails, to his *gada* class. Thus, Legesse notes, "on a limited scale, Borana has the characteristics of a pluralistic society." (Legesse, pp. 209–23.)

Limited or not, it is this sort of pluralism that is antithetical to the artificial, monolithic one-partyism, with its autocratic monopoly of power and patronage, that some African leaders, on the extremes of both right and left, are attempting to impose on their peoples. The *gada* system survived the imperial rule of Haile Selassie, and it survives today under the Marxist government in Addis Ababa because, Legesse told me, the current leftist military officers "have no understanding of, or interest in, the traditional democratic institutions" of the country, regarding them as residues of a feudal past bound to wilt away in time.

Across the southern Ethiopian border, other authors have noted the role of age-sets in the traditional processes of Kenyan tribes. Among the Maasai, "elder age-grades comprised the traditional administrative bodies." They "have had neither headmen nor chiefs" and instead of a coercive authority "public opinion based on custom coerced."

The Samburu possessed no headmen until the British colonial government appointed them in the 1920s, reducing the influence of the council of elders. (See Andrew Fedders and Cynthia Salvadori, *Peoples and Culture of Kenya*. Nairobi: Transafrica, 1984.)

Women among the Elgeyo participated in the election of the *kirukindet*, the advisor who presided over the *kokuet* or council of leaders. Councils on all levels were found among the Embu, dominating the decision-making process within the generation age-sets. The elaborate hierarchical council structure is described by Fedders as follows:

The most basic and localized unit was the family with the father as head; next came the settlement or ridge council with the elders of a locality participating. After that came the clan council with the *athamaki*, the elders versed in clan traditions and possessing influence participating.

Above all these were the *Njama ya ita*, the council of warrior leaders, and *Ciama*, the councils of justice; and the highest authority was *Kiama kia Ngome*, dispensing justice of all kinds, settling disputes, and calling upon the lesser councils to execute its decisions. Binding all together, however, were the generation age-sets, which made and proclaimed laws governing behavior and social practice. They were the repository of ritual practice as well. (Fedders and Salvadori, p. 122.)

The most strikingly democratic people in Kenya appears to be the Kikuyu through whom "one is able to detect, in microcosm, two features of life which are characteristic of contemporary Kenya: a basically egalitarian, democratic political system; and a productive, expanding free market system of economy." Fedders' enthusiasm brings him to contrast Kenya's democratic traditions with "the kind of coercive, despotic, authoritarian, bloodthirsty kingdom... typical of West Africa, as well as of Uganda and Ethiopia." (Fedders and Salvadori, p. 119.)

Despite Fedders' dim view of West Africa, egalitarian democracy has not been limited to East African cultures alone. It was, in fact, on the West Coast of Africa, at the beginning of the eighteenth century, that a European term, current today, was first applied to people's assemblies: *palaver*, directly from the Portuguese *palavra*, meaning speech or talk. (Joseph Kasule, "Palaver and Its Influence in Current Constitutional and International Law, Ph.D. diss., University of Cologne, 1972.)

"To the Portuguese, the people's assemblies on the West Coast of Africa in which anything of interest to an African was talked about, were Palavers," writes Kasule. The legendary Englishman Stanley found the institutions in other parts of Africa, and Kasule sums up its now familiar characteristics:

> They were institutions of one or several villages in which elders sat under a tree and talked until they came to an agreement. In such meetings public affairs were discussed, business was carried on, law suits were brought up, cases settled, and the like. Even a small matter could bring about heated words, in which each one present has the right to express his opinion freely. (Kasule, p. 6.)

Palaver operates in an "African traditional society characterized by the prevalence of the idea of community. The group takes precedence over the individual. Though there is a well-ordered graduation between persons who command and who obey, yet the prevailing feeling is that of equality." (Kasule, p. 6.)

The substantive as well as the formal rules that govern the palaver are embodied in exactly that "cake of custom" which we have examined in previous chapters. Kasule gives useful detail of it, citing first a Western authority and then offering his own African viewpoint:

These rules are of no mysterious origin. Many have developed in society as a result of the product of economic activities, while others derive their existence from the authority of precedents or from voluntary jurisdiction or from deliberate enactment. All these rules of conduct embody the ways of life which have grown up within; or have been enacted by the community, and to a greater extent, each class of rules implies a judgment upon action or behavior. (Quoted by Kasule from *Notes and Queries on Anthropology*, 5th ed. London: Committee of the Royal Anthropological Institute of Great Britain and Ireland, 1929, p. 142.)

This is applicable not only to the African traditional society but also to the world community whose law is not set by a parliament but rather develops slowly from the behavior and activities of nations. The laws are simply there and as one grows up in society, he is taught how to behave according to custom. How is social order maintained in a community without fixed laws? Various forms of social pressure, egality and the spirit of togetherness serve to maintain law and order. Neighbors and relatives depend on each other for help in many undertakings, so there is an incentive to cooperate with one another. (Kasule, p. 8.)

However, the free spirit of palaver has been manipulated by one-party leaders and military dictators who have, Kasule writes, sought to appear "to introduce it on the national level, yet moving away from democracy to dictatorship," ignoring that true palaver is not possible without pluralist opinion. Kasule explained that the young African elite were favoring dictatorship "having been impressed by China's rapid advance." He was writing in 1972, some years before China's leaders finally admitted the failure of monolithic socialism and rushed into liberation of the economy, if not yet of the society.

In Nigeria, the most populous nation of West Africa, the constitutional government was once more replaced with military rule on December 31, 1983. Hugh P. Elliott, an Englishman with thirty-three years of experience (1934–1967) as colonial administrative officer in that country and with more years of close acquaintance in retirement as a Moral Re-Armament representative in Ethiopia, Kenya, and Zimbabwe, does not accept the lament from the West that Nigerian democracy is dead.

"Nigerians are so passionately democratic," he told me at a meeting in India shortly after the year-end coup in Lagos, "and the soldiers know that they will become so unpopular as to make government impossible if they try to establish a dictatorship." He thought at the time that although the Nigerian press was curbed it was still largely free, that the independence of the judiciary had been maintained and that arrests, though massive, were directed only against leading politicians and not at ordinary citizens. He attributed the effective popular resistance to full dictatorship to the inherent democratic characters of the leading tribes embraced by the republic.

For the present study he agreed to write down personal notes on four of these tribes, a sort of eyewitness account in language not inhibited by the professional discipline of the anthropologist:

> The following examples of different forms of African democracy at work that I have personally witnessed are all taken from Nigeria; but I have noticed very similar features in other parts of Africa such as Ghana, Kenya, and Zimbabwe:
>
> 1. The Idoma, a vigorous people in the Benue State of the Middle Belt of Nigeria. Years ago we administered this wild and little-known area of thick orchard bush through "Warrant Chiefs." But we found that these chiefs were little more than spokesmen for the clan/Districts they represented.
>
> The real source of power lay elsewhere. We were required by the British Governor to make detailed studies and to prepare reports on the tribal organization in each District. I personally spent many weeks in bush holding innumerable meetings with chiefs, elders and people to learn all I could about their history, genealogy, clan and family structure, marriage customs, dances, legends, etc. (They were cooperative and we had many interesting and amusing discussions—at one point the elders asked me to tell them about my genealogy!)
>
> I found—as did my colleagues who made similar reports on other

sections of the tribe—that although there were variations, and in some areas there was a powerful personality who took most of the decisions, the source of power rested with a group of elders. These would be the senior representatives of a clan who could trace their ancestry back to a single individual, usually ten or more generations back.

Any issue affecting the tribe was discussed in public—any adult male could attend. After noisy and often heated discussion, sometimes lasting many hours, or days, the elders would arrive at a consensus view and the senior of them would announce the decision.

It was a genuinely democratic process. The minority whose views were not accepted might go away with loud protests. But once the consensus had been reached and the decision announced, woe betide any individual who disobeyed, or who intrigued against it. The penalties were ruthless. "Excommunication" from all festivals and clan activities were enough to bring rebels to heel.

2. The Jukon tribe, also in the Middle Belt of Nigeria, is situated some three hundred miles northeast of the Idomas. They were a theocratic society, with a long history and traditions, having once ruled an empire stretching over considerable areas of what are now Benue and Gongola States. At their head was a priest-chief, the *Aku*. Elaborate rituals surrounded him. He gave the final decisions but he had a council of priests and elders of which he was largely the mouthpiece.

The special feature of this tribe was that it had evolved a system whereby no *Aku*, ruler of an Empire, could become too powerful. Their priest-chief was ceremonially killed after holding office for seven years and another elected to take his place. When I was there in the 1930s, the *Aku*'s predecessor had been disposed of in this way, and the British District Officer was anxiously working out how he could prevent the same thing happening to the existing *Aku*, a good man whom we had got to know well. The practice has long since been abandoned, and no modern Jukon wants to revive it, but the strong democratic tradition has been preserved.

3. The Kano Emirate, some five hundred miles north of the Jukon, a totally different area of climate and thought. The Fulani kingdoms of northern Nigeria were established by a *jihad* (holy war) in a Muslim revival some one hundred fifty years ago, in which the corrupt Hausa kingdoms established hundreds of years before were conquered. When the area was taken over by the British in 1902, we found a well-organized system of administration, with a ruling Emir, councillors each with his own title and function, District Heads administering districts and with a village-head in charge of each village.

We allowed the system to continue by "indirect rule" and did little more than adapt it to modern needs (taxation, etc.), stop slave-raiding and the excesses of corruption and cruel practices. In appearance the Emir was supreme head; and in certain cases in previous history powerful men had ruled autocratically. But in practice the checks and balances that had been evolved made it a much more democratic system than it appeared. The Emir took decisions only after they had been fully discussed in Council. He was himself chosen by a Council of State which normally followed the old tradition (common in many parts of Africa) of choosing a suitable man from one of three or four leading families in rotation.

The British administration worked steadily to make the position of the Emir more and more that of a "constitutional monarch." Since independence the Emir's powers have been much more radically curtailed. There is an elected House of Assembly (or was until the recent coup) and the Emir has virtually no executive powers, but still carries with his prestige considerable influence.

4. The Ibo tribe is in southeastern Nigeria (among whom I was working for most of the years 1951–1967). They are originally forest peoples, who grew from a number of clans in competitive rivalry to a population of over ten million in 1967 (and today at least sixteen million); and they are one of the most vigorous, democratic and educationally advanced peoples in all Africa.

Their social system never permitted any chiefs. Each community, clan or sub-clan takes its decisions in open discussion in their meeting place under the forest trees. As with the Idoma, the final authority rests with a group of elders in the senior "age-grade" and decisions are reached after a consensus. (I am describing the traditional system; today it has been modified by elected District Councils.)

At the time when I was District Officer of an Ibo Division on the Cross River, the people had become enthusiastic about Community Development. To build a motor road to their own village, or a bridge, or a primary school, or a maternity clinic was the aim of each community. Funds were short and the Administration could only provide materials like cement and expert supervision. Their labour was provided free and would turn out en masse—men, women and children—to clear the bush and bring sand and stone.

To assist them with this work I held many meetings with the people. Questions would be put and the alternatives discussed. (On one occasion when I had some overseas guests with me they wondered if they should run for cover before sticks and spears started to fly.) After some time there would be a sudden silence. To the astonishment of any white visitor, the senior elder would announce that they had decided on X. Thereafter, everyone had to turn out to work on that project and fines were imposed, or other penalties, on any defaulter.

Deafening noise during formal deliberations is something not unusual to Western ears that have had occasion to tune in on the freewheeling style of the British House of Commons. However, ceremonially killing a chief at the end of his seven-year term as a check on the abuse of power, a kind of determined, macabre democracy, might seem to be a bit much, even for the most passionate democrat. It constituted erring on the side, as it were, of virtue.

The Nigerian president deposed in the 1983 coup, Alhaji Shehu Shagari, in a speech read before the Conference on Free Elections held in Washington, D.C., in November, 1982, spoke of a less bloody but just as effective traditional Nigerian method for disposing of tyrants. "In some Emirates," he said, "the residence of the ruler had another gate at the rear. In the event that the people had considered a ruler to be dictatorial, the local warriors would assemble in front of his residence to shout advice to him or her to abdicate, the failure of which would result in his or her forceable removal. The wise ruler exited quickly through the rear gate."

The former president also recalled that the chiefs and emirs of Nigeria were, in each instance, "made" by traditional kingmakers, leaders representing scholarship, military prowess, arts, crafts, and agriculture, who could never themselves aspire to become rulers, but who selected "from a large number of eligible candidates whose qualifications consist not only of direct descendency of the deceased ruler or his kins, but also the best rulership qualities in terms of political and religious leadership," surely a superior and more democratic test for kingship than the accident, as in traditional European kingdoms, of being the eldest child of the deceased monarch.

"It is thus clear," Shagari asserted, "that African traditional heritage is basically democratic by nature," and, therefore, he found it "enigmatic and contradictory that some African States operate one-party systems of government." If one might polish up an American catch-all popular in the anticommunist 1950s, one-party systems are, in fact, terribly un-African.

Shagari was also relieved that "years of colonization by Europeans did not affect the basic democratic nature of the traditional system," a comforting thought which is shared by the former colonial official Elliott, who concludes his notes observing that "throughout the continent Africans long to preserve the fundamental freedoms, the democratic roots are still there." In a century of "revisionism," for instance, against orthodox Marxism as well as orthodox theology, this revisionist view is perhaps the most startling and the most reassuring of all: The West may have scattered precious institutional forms for free democratic expression and development all over the world—but let there also be joy that the West did not succeed in destroying the original substantive democracy of non-Western societies.

19 Semitic Pluralism

The year 1492 is remembered as the year a Genoese adventurer sailing under the flag of Catholic Spain stumbled onto the New World. It is not always remembered as also the year of the fall of the Kingdom of Granada, the last Moorish outpost on Spanish soil. Thenceforth Islam, whose legions had occupied most of Spain for eight centuries, was to recede eastward, to become a permanently non-Western phenomenon, leaving Christianity unchallenged as the sole religious base for the political philosophy of the West.

Western perception of Islamic culture and politics tends to equate it with Arabic-Persian reality, ignoring the massive Muslim presence beyond West Asia. Thus, Muslim scholars such as Hussein Alatas complain that there is not enough separation in the Western mind of "what is essentially Islamic and what is specifically the elements of particular cultures whose societies are predominantly Muslims." (Hussein Alatas, *The Democracy of Islam*. The Hague: W. Van Hoeve, 1956, p. 5.)

Alatas points out as a good example "the separation of women and the use of veils by them," an "Arabic-Persian custom" which "many writers have confused with the teaching of Islam." (Alatas, p. 8.) The Hollywood image of obscenely wealthy sheikhs making, in between ceremonial salaams toward Mecca, obsequious subjects jump at the snap of bejeweled fingers has induced fanciful visions of Islam as an exotic theological base for absolute, despotic power.

Professor Abdul Aziz Said, who is Syrian and teaches international relations at American University in Washington, D.C., and his colleague Jamil Nasser, a Muslim scholar, while not insisting that "democracy, Western or Islamic, is practiced in the present Muslim world," dispute "the assertion by certain Western scholars and practitioners that the Muslim world is not ready for democracy." (Note: During 1979–1980 Professor Said, Professor Brady Tyson, a Methodist minister once associated with U.S. Ambassador Andrew Young, and myself jointly taught a course in world democracy at American University.) They dismiss it as "a perspective that sees democracy as only a form." They could be referring to American writers like George F. Kennan, whom we saw earlier falling into the same error, when they lament that "for many years, scholars have equated Western institutional forms of democracy with the substance of democracy." (Jack Nelson and Vera Green, eds., *International Human Rights: Contemporary Issues*. Standforville, N.Y.: Earl Cloeman Enterprises, 1980, p. 61.)

"The substance of democracy," Said and Nasser propose, expanding on the original dictionary definition we saw in Chapter 1, "is a human society that has a sense of common goals, a sense of community, a process of participation in making decisions, and protective safeguards for dissenters." This is to be distinguished from the "form of democracy [which] is cast in the mold of the culture of a people." (Nelson and Green, p. 61.)

There is a difference between not practicing democracy for lack of preparation for it, and not practicing it in spite of being prepared for it by historical, cultural, and religious traditions. If democracy is difficult to identify among Islamic peoples today, it is because Islamic democratic traditions, for either domestic or international geopolitical reasons, are not being practiced.

There are as many precepts in Islamic law as there are in those of the other great religions which preach those ideals best encapsulized in the French trinity—liberty, equality, fraternity. There are also Islamic traditions, as there have been in other great religions, which in practice result in transgressions against those ideals.

In the end, as Said and Nasser conclude, "democracy is built upon participation, not institutions." It is the participation of the people that can change a bad law, a corrupt custom, a distorted interpretation.

The Muslim Divine Law, the Shariah, is the fountain of four essential freedoms, those of the person, of expression, of religious belief, and of private ownership. The Prophet Muhammad is quoted in his profound advocacy of individual freedom: "The best *jihad* [holy war] is a word of truth before an authoritarian leader," as direct an exhortation to challenge dictatorship as has been uttered by a founder of a major religion. Also, if the protection of private property will appeal to the conservative U.S. Republican, there is also the redistributive precept to please the liberal Democrat, the institution of *zakat* or compulsory contributions to the poor in the society. (Nelson and Green, pp. 75–76.)

It was the sense of popular participation, however, that guaranteed the implementation of these egalitarian precepts in the early days of Islamic polity. The structure for this participation was principally the Shura, a consultative mechanism which was "a prerequisite for the functioning of the political system." Its purpose was "to enhance the role of the community in decision-making and provide individuals with the opportunity to participate in the governing process." The consultation was guided by three rules: "(1) participation was an inherent right of both the people and their leader, and none had priority over the other; (2) the deliberation of all community affairs must take place in the consultative assembly, and the ruler is required to submit affairs to consultation, for the Quran [holy book] states: 'and consult them in affairs (of moment)'; and (3) faith and sincerity must accompany any consultation." (Nelson and Green, p. 68.) The condition of "faith and sincerity" operates to exclude from discussion matters regulated by the Quran, a safeguard against heresy which persists even today in various forms of Christian churches.

Hindu scholar Radhakamal Mukerjee, who belonged to a

culture for which Islam has been a fierce historical rival, views the Muslim consultative process in the context of the traditional Arab sheikhdoms, once more censuring rash Western perceptions of Islamic society:

> Western scholars have accustomed us to identify the development of Islamic polity with the pomp and grandeur of the courts of the Ommiad and Abbasid Caliphs. The Semitic conception of a republican State finds but little notice, and yet the communal-democratic system of politics, founded upon the basis of theocracy in the Islamic commonwealth, is one of the most remarkable phenomena of political evolution, not less significant than the development of the Athenian democracy and the Roman republic.
>
> In the social organization of the nomads and the settled Arabs, sheikhs or heads of clans and families administered tribal affairs, and were guided by the customary laws of the clans and the *gens*. All matters affecting the community were discussed in the *majlis* or assembly of elders. The council of elders of the ancient Arabs ultimately developed into the national council.
>
> After the death of Muhammad, his companions administered the law as they had received it from the Prophet, but all cases of doubt and difficulty were solved by the *ijma*, i.e., consensus of opinion or general accord. For the purpose there were two councils—the national council and the council of citizens.
>
> Important matters affecting the State or community in general used to be referred to the national council (*nmajlis-i-shura*), when all the companions of the Prophet and the chief men of the tribes were invited. Matters of less importance were referred to the council of the citizens, where the *mhajirins* and *ansars*, i.e., the Meccan and Medinite companions that happened to be present in the town, used to assemble, and the point in issue was decided by their consent. The consent of either of the two councils was necessary for all measures. (Radhakamal Mukerjee, *Democracies of the East*. New Delhi: 1923, p. 174.)

Mukerjee is careful to sort out the Islamic and the Semitic (Arabic) components of this republican democracy:

> The democratic spirit of the Islamic law corresponded with the Semitic idea of a republican State and with the large measure of freedom and independence that were still reserved for local bodies, tribal councils, and communal assemblies. (Mukerjee, p. 175.)

Popular participation in Islamic polity originally extended to the choice of the *Khalifa* (Caliph), the supreme leader who was chosen by election and formally accepted by the people in a process called *Bay'ah*. (Nelson and Green, p. 62.) It was the Shiites, supporters of "Ali, son-in-law of the Prophet Muhammad," who introduced the concept of hereditary succession, initiating within Islam an authoritarian tradition which today prevails among 10 percent of the entirety of the Islamic world, including Iran.

Where democratic elections were abolished, many of the people moved elsewhere to regions where the right was still guaranteed. Mukerjee reports that "when the old Arab franchise, which was a universal franchise, disappeared and the right to elect the sovereign fell into the hands of the soldiery and the inhabitants of the capital, a portion of the Arab population passed over to the Kharijite camp, where the old democratic ideas prevailed." (Mukerjee, pp. 170–71.) These stubbornly free people preferred a land "where even the necessity for and usefulness of a head of the State was called into question and denied, or where the election of the sovereign was held to be wholly unfettered by any consideration of hereditary succession or family connection, for they maintained that even a slave or a peasant, if just and pious, was eligible for sovereignty." (Mukerjee, pp. 170–71.)

The original republican caliphate conducted public affairs along "rightly ordered constitutional lines." Judicial work was entrusted to city councils, presided over by the town *qazis* and *muftis*, as well as the corporations of merchants, presided over by the *rais-ul-tujjar*. Everyone had access to mosques during decisions of cases by the *caliph*, the *kadis*, and *nain-kadis*, assisted by *adls*.

The veil-covered, second-class status of women in some West Asian Muslim societies today is not representative of the body of original Islamic egalitarian practices, such as that of appointing female jurists and judges, for "a woman can be, under the Islamic law, a jurist and a judge, can appear in a lawsuit before a *kadi* and plead her cause, can act as a ... magistrate, can hear appeals and decide cases on reference." (Mukerjee, p. 175.)

This may not be the reality in most of the Islamic world today, but we are here dealing not necessarily with the present but with the truth about the traditional past. Said and Nasser, surveying today's thirty-six Islamic states, find that two-thirds of them are under military or quasi-military regimes, and one-third under absolute or near absolute hereditary systems. Only fourteen of them practice some form of universal suffrage. Saudi Arabia, the United Arab Emirates, and Kuwait "have Shura councils ostensibly modeled after Islamic precepts," but "these councils do not function." In some countries where the Muslims are in the majority, there have been some faltering gains, in at least one case, that of Turkey, through secularization, i.e., divorcing government from Islamic polity. In Malaysia, the limitations on the democratic experiment appear to be dictated by the peculiar balance of population between Malays, Chinese, and Indians, which was an explosive colonial legacy from the British.

In West Asia and North Africa, the pressures on Islamic nations coming from forces and realities far and near may be driving them to reaction and a consequent reactionary interpretation of their original religious ethic. One of these proximate realities is Israel.

I experienced the dynamic and self-confidence of tiny Israel, which make its neighbors uneasy, when I visited it as a guest of the late Golda Meir. It all comes from its being both a deeply rooted religious nation and a modern democracy. The political leadership of that democracy has been educated primarily in Britain and continental Europe. (I was accompanied by a British-accented Israeli diplomat, Shaul Ramati, to see the renowned David Ben-Gurion, who spoke English with a Russian accent, and Mrs. Ben-Gurion, who had a Brooklyn accent.) The population itself is made up primarily of immigrants from Europe. However, to attribute to this European and British heritage alone the continuing success of Israel's democracy would not be far from perpetuating that historic bias with which Jewish culture has been judged by the European Christian.

Indeed, the culture of Europe, developed out of the Judeo-Christian ethic, is partly Jewish. Millions of Jews, too, have populated Europe, and persecution and prejudice drove them to develop their own Hebraic polity within the European political reality. Although it was independent of that reality, however, it had to accept the impact of Western Christian institutions. It is only now in Israel that the Jewish faith regains its full identity as a non-Western, West Asian ethic.

The creed of universal human equality finds its first and, to return to Thomas Jefferson's language, most "self-evident" argument in the creationism of the Jewish Bible, the Old Testament of the Christian faith, whose story of Adam as the first human being is believed by the Muslims as well. Springing from these initial "equalizing" creationist lines of Genesis, thousands of biblical precepts counseling justice, freedom, and equality, illustrated with example, parable, and fact from the history of the Jewish people, were written down for the edification first of the Jews and then of the whole of humankind. Many modern writers have analyzed them from a secular point of view, some identifying elements of democracy in the Pentateuch, the Prophecies, and in the Talmud. (See Naomi Ben-Asher, *Democracy's Hebrew Roots*. New York: Hadassah, 1951.)

The parliamentary rules of procedure in the Knesset may read more like a manual from the British Parliament, but much of the substance of modern Israeli democracy may be traced to Jewish historical practice.

In the Talmudic Era, the rise of the Synagogue as an institution in the community was a significant democratic development. It required no indispensable functionary or leader, provided for a working quorum (*minyan*) of ten men, was a house not only of worship but of study open to all. The era also produced what might have been two of the earliest political parties in history.

The conservative view was sustained by the Sadducees, the party of the lay and priestly nobility, the wealthy landowners, and the minor provincial gentry. They were "often autocratic and oppressing absentee landholders," and "they were static in their interpretation of the Torah." Like some modern fundamentalists in other religions, the Sadducees "rejected completely the authority of the oral tradition," which was "a dynamic process of adapting the ancient Torah to a changing society." (Ben-Asher.)

The "progressive" or "liberal" party was that of the Pharisees, an identity which unfortunately was to acquire the connotation of hypocrisy in an isolated passage in the New Testament. The Pharisees were largely "middle class craftsmen, artisans, laborers and merchants," and they "drew their inspiration from the whole stream of prophetic teachings of justice, of human dignity and equality." They were egalitarians, who "emphasized the 'all' in [the biblical passage] 'God hath given unto all as an heritage the kingdom, the priesthood, and the sanctuary.' " (Ben-Asher, p. 34.)

Eventually, the Pharisees' position prevailed, but they were soon themselves divided into a liberal wing, the *maykil*, and a conservative, the *machmir*. Disputes occasioned by these contrasting philosophies were resolved in accordance with "the democratic character of the talmudic period," not by force, but "by bringing to bear the weight of authority, by precedent, and by voice vote." *Yachid verabim—halachah kerabim*, went the rule: "When the majority opposes the opinion of one, the rule is according to the majority." The minority suffered no consequences for its stand. (Ben-Asher, p. 35.)

After the Diaspora, the Jews developed strong local autonomy where power rested "with the council of elders apparently elected by the various congregations of the city." Socially embattled in Europe, they organized country-wide councils where representatives of individual communities were elected by secret ballot, voice vote, or by casting lots—a duplication of sortition, which was popular in Greek democracy. Their resolutions, *takkanot*, were binding upon the represented communities. The most notable of these councils, the *Vaad Arbah Aratzot*—the Council of Four Lands—uniting Jews from four major Polish provinces, enacted *takkanot*, which guaranteed free elections of communal officers and rabbis, and regulated even such matters as unfair competition between communities. (Ben-Asher, p. 54.)

If one looks hard enough, one can find among the sublime precepts in any civilization some incredibly absurd concessions to the principle of equality. Among the reformist measures introduced by the Jewish Pharisees to meet the demand to liberalize the status of women was one forcing a man to grant his wife a divorce "if he is a gatherer of dog's dung, or a copper-smelter, or a tanner, whether these conditions obtained before marriage or they arose after marriage." (Ben-Asher, p. 43.) In American society today, some elements of the United Mine Workers or some affiliates of the AFL-CIO engaged in special services might be expected to resist such a reform as reverse discrimination against the male of the species.

Yet, it is not the absurdity of this law, which in the context of its time may have made some sense, that should impress us. It is rather what it demonstrates: the extremes to which a society can be tempted to go to satisfy the anxiety for human equality, and to countervail the opposite extremes of savage cruelty of which human beings from both West and East—Christian, Muslim, Jew, Hindu, or Buddhist—have historically been found to be so eminently capable.

20 Korea and Japan—the "Improbable Democracies"?

With the discussion on Semitic pluralism we have closed the circle in our survey of indigenous non-Western democratic traditions which began with early Mesopotamia, except for an important gap which we left unclosed on purpose—a region occupied by two interacting nations, Japan and Korea. Although the former is currently a working democracy and the latter is struggling to regain its own, both countries, for reasons based on a superficial appreciation of their history, are often regarded as "improbable democracies."

At this writing crucial events are taking place in that region related to the debate on the universality of the democratic value, and assessing the odds on these nations' hopes for democracy might make a fitting conclusion to our study.

In February, 1985, I traveled to Seoul as part of a delegation of sympathizers accompanying the South Korean democratic leader Kim Dae Jung on his return from U.S. exile. The summary execution of Philippine Senator Benigno Aquino at the Manila International Airport in August, 1983, as he was returning from his own U.S. exile had prompted Kim's supporters to organize a peaceful security cordon around him to protect him from a similar fate.

Along with several members of the twenty-person delegation and some accompanying newsmen, I was still inside the airplane when the scuffling that was seen around the world took place at the end of the debarkation ramp. A phalanx of plainclothes South Korean police charged at Kim, his wife, and the delegation leaders, seeking to separate them with the use of brute force when a simple verbal explanation that it was, as the South Korean government would later claim, just a security precaution might have sufficed. Thus, after traveling halfway around the world, I missed seeing what turned out to be the most celebrated event of our mission.

However, I did not miss seeing what I thought ought to have been regarded as the most significant accomplishment of Kim's return—the turning out by the hundreds of thousands of Kim's sympathizers at the airport and along the avenues leading to downtown Seoul. All of them were cruelly deprived of the satisfaction of even catching a quick glimpse of Kim, who was whisked through side streets to house arrest at his modest home.

The crowds had to be content with watching us in the delegation bus drive by. We could hear them shout anxiously, "Where is Kim? Is he behind you or ahead of you?" Their placards read: "Welcome home, Kim!" "Long live Korean democracy!"

A few years back, the U.S. Ambassador to South Korea had characterized Koreans seeking the restoration of their democracy as "spoiled brats." The commander of American forces stationed in that country was more specific: "Koreans are like field mice, they just follow whoever becomes their leader. Democracy is not an adequate system for Koreans." (Quoted by Bruce Cumins, the *New York Times* opinion editorial, July 6, 1982.) Neither the ambassador nor the general, wrote University of Washington professor Bruce Cumins in the *New York Times*, "understand the centrality of the Kwangju rebellion."

Bordering China, it was inevitable that Koreans become suffused in Confucianism, which we have seen to have been mistakenly equated with absolute conformism. However, unlike most mainland Chinese, South Koreans have not been content with wall posters in their nonconformist struggle for democracy.

Kim Dae Jung's arrest in May, 1980, provoked instant popular reaction throughout the country, the most militant and numerous taking place in the fourth largest city, Kwangju. Suddenly confronted with defiant human beings, the American commanding general who had compared Koreans to follow-the-leader-mice was quick to act. He released South Korean paratroop units under his command that were swiftly flown and dropped into the protest area. When it was over, the soldiers had killed close to 3,000 unarmed civilians. "It made," wrote Cumins, "the suppression of Solidarity in Poland seem like child's play."

Why would Korean "spoiled brats" and "field mice" turn out in such numbers for democracy? Why would they die for such an alien value?

Democratic ideals "are not unique to the West," Kim Dae Jung declared at Harvard University. "The quest for these democratic ideals has been pervasive in Korean history." At a seminar at Columbia University in September, 1983, he recalled the pre-Confucian Dangun mythology which "prescribes that the purpose of governing is to 'greatly benefit the people.'" (Kim Dae Jung, "Democratic Aspects of Korean Tradition." The Korean Seminar, Columbia University, September 16, 1983, p.10.) This gave rise to the "people-first principle" which became "firmly embedded in the national psyche" and provided the fundamental creed for the indigenous Donghak religion which taught that "to serve man is to serve heaven." (Kim, Korean Seminar, p. 10.)

This religion, in turn, furnished the spiritual drive for the Donghak Peasant Revolution of 1894 whose democratic goals were "land redistribution, modification of a rigid class system, emancipation of slaves, permission for widows to remarry, expurgation of corrupt government officials, and popular participation in local government." (Kim, Korean Seminar, p. 11.)

The cry for popular participation was not just of nineteenth century coinage. During the fourth century Silla Dynasty, the Korean people had participated directly in community decision-making through the Hwaback system, which Kim finds "comparable to the direct democracy of the Greek city-states." In the fifth century Silla and Paekjae dynasties, the Namdung system was developed, which produced consensus in government by open discussion between monarchs and officials. Freedom of expression was a reality protected by law during the 500 years of the Yi Dynasty. Although, like the privileges of the nobility in medieval England and continental Europe, this freedom was guaranteed only to the aristocratic Yangban class, comprising about 10 percent of the population, provisions were made to afford the common people the opportunity to voice appeals and complaints directly to the monarch. Taejong, the third king of the Yi Dynasty, began this tradition by placing a drum in front of the royal palace that anyone could beat when he wanted to be heard by the king.

For those beyond the ear of the king, there was applied what we have already seen to be the universal rule made inevitable by the sheer inability of a central monarch to govern every community in his realm due to primitive communications: let them govern themselves. The Yi Dynasty devised the Hangyak system of local autonomy where the art of popular consensus was developed at the village level. "In spite of corruption and incompetence at high government levels," Kim asserts, "local villages functioned smoothly thanks to this system."

To climax his thesis on the potential for a viable Korean democracy, Kim asks: "If one argues that Korean tradition has prevented the development of democracy in Korea, then how does one explain what has happened in Japan since World War II? I believe Japanese tradition is far more authoritarian and militaristic than Korean." (Kim, Korean Seminar, p. 12.)

Kim's critical comparative view of Japanese political tradition may reflect instinctively some of the intense Korean resentment of the harsh Japanese occupation of their homeland. It is also the popular view from the world outside Japan, particularly among Chinese and Southeast Asians who felt the direct impact of Japanese militarism in World War II.

The current democratic reality in Japan, apparently there to stay, puzzles those who perceive emperor-worship, submissiveness to authority, and centralized repression as the only recognizable political characteristics in Japanese culture. Some regard it as "instant democracy," a twentieth-century marvel attributable exclusively to the decisive decrees of Gen. Douglas

MacArthur who, like a god from Olympus, willed it to "his people," bequeathing them a democratic constitution whether they liked it or not.

The fact, of course, is that the Japanese leaders, and people, willed it, too. The Japanese, castigated in defeat, weary of war and penitently admitting guilt for it, themselves wanted democracy and, indeed, a constitution that would ensure that their nation would never go to war again.

But did the Japanese take to democracy out of sheer repentance? And how real is Japanese democracy today?

I had occasion to look in some depth into Japanese politics and political tradition a few years ago when I did a study of the political implications of the Japanese economic presence in Southeast Asia for the Carnegie Endowment for International Peace. (See Raul S. Manglapus, *Japan in Southeast Asia: Collision Course*, New York: Carnegie Endowment for International Peace, 1976.) I found that Japanese democracy is different—but it is real. It is different because beneath the parliamentary institutions partly introduced by the MacArthur constitution and partly carried over from the seventy-year, pre-World War II, post-Meiji reform period (when they were almost always manipulated by the militarists) there is a thick layer of ritualism which is persistent and will probably never disappear.

In my study I wrote of several instances in which this ritualism manifests itself in the new democracy, one of the most amusing of which is the labor movement:

> Tourists in the spring are treated to a unique spectacle in hotels and restaurants. At the Imperial Hotel in Tokyo, if one is lucky enough to register on the right day, one will see all the hotel help, including head waiters, wearing arm bands with such pugnacious slogans as "It's a bad company and we are on strike!" All the while, however, they are serving the customers with the usual smile, bow, and dispatch. For they are only on symbolic strike. Nobody ever really stops working because they expect to work for the Imperial for the rest of their lives, and they will not allow the rival Okura Hotel to profit at the Imperial's expense.
>
> A Maoist delegate at a conference in Tokyo, reports McRae [a writer for the London *Economist*], witnessed a demonstration in a park and

called it "the most exciting thing since Paris in May, 1968." He was shocked to find the next day that it was not headlined in the Tokyo press. Another witness who spoke Japanese understood why. He saw all the demonstrators give their names and the name of their union to the police as they entered the park. Inside the park "they wound headbands round their forehead, unpacked shields and weapons, made the ritual gestures." Then they packed things away, carefully cleared the litter, and filed out. (Manglapus, pp. 33–34.)

Japan is a "vertical society," all of its institutions influenced by the original household *ie*, which, in contrast to the traditional family, including the extended version in many Asian societies, is, according to noted Japanese anthropologist Chie Nakane, a "social group constructed on the basis of an established frame of residence and often of management organization." (Chie Nakane, *Japanese Society*. London: Penguin, 1973, p. 4.)

Under this system, the son-in-law who lives in the same household becomes more important than the son who has left to found his own household. Outsiders with not the remotest kinship may be invited to join the household and become heirs or successors, and servants and clerks living in the household are treated as family members.

"What is important here," Nakane observes, "is that the human relationships within this household group are thought of as more important than all other human relationships." (Nakane, p. 5.) Within the *ie*, seniority of residence, not kinship, and consequently a lifetime commitment became the sacred rule.

In the selective modernization undertaken by the Meiji restoration in the 1870s, the structure and spirit of the *ie*, with its traditions of seniority and lifetime commitment, were built into the new institutions, including the industrial and commercial enterprises. Thus, one of the early companies, the Japanese National Railway, was called *Kokutetsu-ikka*, which literally means "one railway family."

All this ritualism can tempt one to doubt the substance, while admiring the forms, of current Japanese democracy. Yet, the *ie* system unobtrusively contains within itself a democratic element which Americans, eager to emulate superior Japanese efficiency, are just now beginning to perceive as an important part of the elusive Japanese secret formula for industrial success. In the traditional *ie*, decisions were reached by consensus after prolonged discussions participated in by every member of the household. It was expected that in the end the basic proposal of the head of the household would prevail, but everyone had the opportunity to contribute and to object. This "household democracy" was transplanted to the industrial enterprise where management and workers periodically engage in prolonged consultations on policies and techniques. American workers and managers employed by Japanese companies in the United States are currently undergoing this new democratic experience and have been reported to be enthusiastic in their praise of the system, not only because it leads to cooperation and efficiency, but also because it has rendered their human dignity a new and meaningful dimension. American management experts are now examining the process for grafting into the American industrial complex itself.

However, the rediscovery of this somewhat esoteric indigenous Japanese consensual tradition is not the only indication of original Japanese participatory democracy. Japanese emperors and feudal lords (*daimyos*) could not claim to be an exception to the inexorable "fate" of the early central ruler— that of having to leave their distant communities to govern themselves due to primitive facilities. "The *daimyos*, or feudal lords of Japan possessed no absolute tenure of the districts over which they ruled." Hence, the paradox that "Japanese political life was dominated by the mystic reverence for the symbolic imperial head, the Mikado, as the pater familias on the one hand, and on the other by the democratic proclivities of rural communities independent in the conduct and administration of municipal affairs." (Radhakamal Mukerjee, *Democracies of the East*. New Delhi, 1923, pp. 187–88.)

Mukerjee details some of these "democratic proclivities":

Formerly, under the *narushi* or *shoya*, elected village headman, there was an honorary official called *kumi-gashira* or *toshiyori*, whose duty was to act in the interest of the farmers. In other places the official called *hyaku-shodai* was elected, and his duty was to negotiate with the headmen on behalf of the villagers in matters relating to public interest. Similarly, in the cities of Japan, as in those in China and India, there were certain officials who discharged important administrative functions within the respected wards under their charge. (Mukerjee, p. 186.)

Mukerjee also referred to a local Japanese "popular assembly" called *kai-goshu*, which managed all judicial and administrative affairs. (Mukerjee, n., p. 187.)

So the "missing link" in the global chain of indigenous non-Western democratic traditions is put in place. The "improbable democracies" are, after all, not that improbable. If Korea (North and South) regains its democracy and Japan's own persists, they will, like other non-Western nations, no doubt draw heavily from Western experiential forms. However, each has an historical, substantial native base on which to build a lasting democracy it can call its own.

In addition, a lasting, indigenous democracy need not be a static one. It could even be permanently revolutionary, for, as American poet Archibald MacLeish has proclaimed, "Democracy is the only valid revolution for the world today."

Index

Aborigines (Australian), 78–79
absolutism vs. pluralism (Mexico), 110–11
adat (Malay customary law), 68–71, 73
Africa: egalitarianism in, 134–35, 137–39; hierarchical systems in, 135, 137; one-party system in, 134–35, 137; tribal governments in, 126–31; Western imperialism in, 125. *See also individual tribes*
Aguirre Beltran, Gonzalo, 111–12, 115
Alaska, 107
Alatas, Hussein, 145
Alexander, King of Macedon, 31–32
Alisjahbana, S. Takdir, 68
Allen, W. M. F., 16–17
apoo (Tahiti), 85–86
Arabic-Persian culture, confusion with Islamic culture, 145–46
archaic civilization, evolution of, 2–10, 13–17
Aryans, 30–31, 38, 48–49

Assyria, 21–22
Australia, 78–79
autocracy vs. democracy, coexistence of, 61–66
Aztecs, 110–17

Babylonia, 22
Bandelier, A. F., 112–16
Bantu (South Africa), 126–31
barangay (Philippine settlement), 71–73
Beauchamp, William M., 95, 97–98
Berlin Conference, 125, 133
Bible (Old Testament), 151
Borana (Ethiopia), 135–37
Britain: class distinctions in, 47–48; colonialism in Burma, 66; colonialism in India, 42–44, 46
Buckley, William F., Jr., 9–10
Buddha (Siddhartha Gautama), 28–29
Burma, 61–66

caste, 49–52
Chesterton, G. K., 3–4, 5

China: class distinctions in, 58; communication systems and terrain, effect on democracy, 7–8; Confucian ethic in, 55–59; family customs of, 56–57; similarities to India, 32; village government in, 54–55
Christian Democratic International (CDI), 133
civil service examinations (China), 57–58
class distinctions: Britain, 47–48; China, 58; India, 48–52
classless society, goal of, 52, 99
Cleveland, Harland, 69, 87
Cola Kingdom of Uttaramerur, 36–38
communication systems, effect on democracy and despotism, 5–8, 32, 158
condescension of West to non-West, 8–10
Confucian ethic, 55–59
consensual system, 158, 160–61; vs. adversarial voting, 68–70; vs. unanimity, 87, 103, 129–30
constitutions, early Indian, 37–38
consultative process (Islamic), 147–49
council meetings (Navaho), 104–7
cultural norms, power of, 13–15
custom, power of, 13–15
customary law: Filipino, 71–73; Malay (*adat*), 68–71, 73; customs vs. statutory law, 15–17

datu (Filipino chieftain), 71–73
de la Costa, Horacio, 6–7, 71
democratic values: autocracy and, 61–66; cavemen and, 1–3, 5; coexistence with despotism, 5–10, 82–83; communication systems, effect on, 5–8, 32, 158; Confucian ethic and, 55–59; consensus voting of, 68–69; evolution of, 3–5, 8–9, 13–17; imperialism's influence on, 43–44; Indian caste relationship to, 51–52; universality of ("natural state of man" concept), 2–5, 7–8, 13–17, 21–23, 25, 30, 33, 76, 80. *See also individual countries*
despotism: coexistence with democracy, 5–10, 82–83; communication systems, effect on, 5–8, 32, 158; evolution of, 3–6; Oriental, 6–10, 19
dissension techniques (Navajo), 106–7
Donghak (Korean religion), 157
Durant, Will, 7

Easter Island, 87–88
Ebla (lost kingdom), 23–24
egalitarianism, 13–15; Africa, 134–35, 137–39; Mesopotamia, 21–23; religion and, 23
Elliott, Hugh P., 139–43
Engels, Friedrich, 98–99
"equivalence" and "strength" (New Guinea), 77–78
Eskimos, 14
Ethiopia, 135–37

Fairbank, John K., 53–54
family customs: China, 56–57; Japan, 160–61
Farb, Peter, 91–92, 98–99
Fedders, Andrew, 137–38
fokon'olona (Malagasy Republic village assembly), 74–75

Index 165

fono (South Sea Island village assembly), 83–87
Fox, Robert, 72–73
France, imperialism in Malagasy Republic, 74–76
Fuentes, Carlos, 109–10
"full belly" theory, 35

Gandhi, Mahatma, 44
Guatama, Siddhartha (Buddha), 28–29
gens: Iroquois ancestral unit, 93–95; Mexican, 112–13
Greek imperialism, in India, 31–32
gumlao (Burma), 62–63
gumsa (Burma), 62–63

Hangyak system (Korea), 158
Han Indians (Alaska), 107
Hearst, William Randolph, Jr., 10
Hiawatha, 96
hierarchical African systems, 135, 137
hierarchism, 15
Horam, Mashangthei, 64–65
Hutton, J. H., 50, 62
"hydraulic society," 6, 19–20

Ibo (Nigeria), 142–43
Idoma (Nigeria), 140–41
ie (Japanese household hierarchy), 16–61
Ikongko (Malagasy Republic), 75
imperialism: British, 42–44, 46, 66; condescension of West in, 8–10; French, 74–76; Greek, 31–32; influence on democratic values, 43–44; Western, in Africa, 125
Incas, 120

India: Aryans, 30–31, 38, 48–49; Britain in, 42–44, 46; Buddha, 28–29; class distinctions in, 48–52; Cola Kingdom, 36–38; constitutions, early, 37–38; Greek imperialism in, 31–32; Licchavis, 27–30; Mauryan Period, 31; Munda-Dravidian culture, 36–39; panchayat of, 41–42, 43–46; political mobilization in, 50–52; raja, 28–29; Sakyas, 28–29; similarities to China, 32; terrain of, effect on democracy in, 32; village assembly, 36–39
Indians, American. *See specific tribe names*
Indo-Aryan polity, 38–39
Iroquois Confederacy, 90–99
Islamic culture, 145–50
Israel, 150–53

Jacobsen, Thorkild, 21–23
Japan, 158–62
Jewish culture, 150–53
Juarez, Benito, 109–10
Jukon (Nigeria), 141

Kano Emirate (Nigeria), 141–42
Kasule, Joseph, 138–39
Kennan, George F., 8–9
Kenya, 137–38
Kikuyu (Kenya), 138
Kim Dae Jung, 155–58
Korea, 156–58
K'ung-fu-tze. *See* Confucian ethic
Kwangju rebellion (Korea), 156–57

Leach, E. R., 62–63
Legesse, Asmarom, 134–37
LeJeune, Jesuit Father, 13–14

Licchavis, 27–30
Linton, Ralph, 74–76
"loyal opposition," 55–57
Luce, Clare Booth, 10

Maasai (Kenya), 137
MacArthur constitution (Japan), 158–59
Malagasy Republic (Madagascar), 74–76
Malays, 67–76
Maoris, 79–80
Marquesas, 86
Marx, Karl: flaw in thinking, 12–13; 15–16; Iroquois Confederacy and, 98–99; perception of India, 42–44; view of proletariat, 12
matriarchy, Iroquois, 91–93, 94–95
Mauryan Period (India), 31
Mayans, 119–20
Menabe (Malagasy Republic), 75
Mencius, 57
Mesopotamia, 20–25
Mexico, 109–17. *See also* Aztecs; Incas; Mayans
monarchy vs. nobility, catalyst for democracy, 52
Morgan, Lewis H., 4–5, 92–97
Mukerjee, Radhakamal, 147–49
Munda-Dravidian culture, 36–38
Muslim Divine Law (Shariah), 147
Muslims, 145–50

Naga, 64–66
Nasser, Jamil, 146–47
Navajos, 106–7
Nepal, 28
New Guinea, 77–80
New Zealand, 79–80

Nigeria, 139–43
Niue, 86–87
nobility vs. monarchy, catalyst for democracy, 52
Nyerere, Julius, 134

Obote, Milton, 133–34
Oglala Sioux (South Dakota), 107
one-party system, mistake of (Africa), 134–35, 137
Oppenheim, A. Leo, 20–21
Orient: despotism in, 6–10, 19; vs. West in political evolution, 5–10. *See also* China; Japan; Korea
ostracism, 122, 124. *See also* withdrawal
Otavalos (Ecuador), 123–24

palavers, 138–39
panchayat, 41–46
Pharisees, 152
Philippines, 71–73
pluralism vs. absolutism (Mexico), 110–11
political mobilization in Indian society, Rudolph theory, 50–52
proletariat: Marxian view of, 12; Toynbee view of, 11–12

rajas (India), 28–29
Read, K. E., 77–78
religion: legends of, and egalitarianism, 23; Maori governmental order and, 80
ritualism (Japan), 159–61
Rotuma (Fiji), 81, 87

sachems (Iroquois clan chief), 92–95
Saducees, 151

Index 167

Said, Abdul Aziz, 146–47
Sakyas, 28–29
Samoa, 82–85
Sapa Inca, 120
Saraguros (Ecuador), 120–22
Service, Elman R., 7, 12–13, 111–12
sexual equality (Navajo), 104
Shans (Burma), 61–66
Shariah (Muslim Divine Law), 147
Shiites, 149
Shuaras (Ecuador), 122–23
Shura (Islamic consultative mechanism), 147
Silla Dynasty (Korea), 157
Sotho (South Africa), 128–29
Soustelle, Jacques, 110–11
South Africa, 125–31
South Sea Islands, 82–88
Spanish conquistadors: conquest of Aztecs, 110–12, 116; influence on Navajo, 104–5; Philippine invasion by, 71–73
statutory law vs. customs, 15–17
Stevenson, H. N. C., 62
"strength" and "equivalence" (New Guinea), 77–78
Sun Yat-sen, 7–8
"Symposium on Traditional Governance in Non-Western Cultures" (1980), 69
Synagogue, 157

Tahiti, 85–86
Taiwan, 53
terrain, effect on village autonomy, 32
Toynbee, Arnold: flaw in thinking, 12–13, 15–16; view of proletariat, 11–12

tribal government (South Africa), 126–31
tribal system (Navajo), 102–7
Tsimihety (Malagasy Republic), 74–75

Uganda, 133–35
unanimity vs. consensus, 87, 103, 129–30
United States Constitution, relation to Iroquois Confederacy, 97–98

Vargas Llosa, Mario, 110
varna, Indian class distinctions, 49
"vertical society" (Japan), 160
village assemblies, 36–39
village government: Burma, 61–66; China, 54–55; India, 36–39; Japan, 162; Malagasy Republic (Madagascar), 74–76; Malay, 68–71; New Guinea, 77–79; Philippines, 71–73; South Sea Island, 83–88

West vs. Orient in political evolution, 5–10
Williams, Aubrey W., 106–7
Wilson, Peter J., 74–76
"withdrawal" (Navajo dissension), 106–7
Wittfogel, Karl, 6, 19–20
women, leaders in Iroquois Confederacy, 91–95

Yi Dynasty (Korea), 158
Young, Robert W., 102, 105
Yuan Chwang, 32–33

Zulu (South Africa), 127–28

About the Author

RAUL S. MANGLAPUS is President of Democracy International and former President (now International Vice-President) of the Center for Development Policy. He is also President of the Christian Social Movement in the Philippines (now National Union of Christian Democrats) and Vice-President of the Christian Democratic International. Prior to leaving the Philippines in 1972, he served as Under Secretary of Foreign Affairs, Secretary of Foreign Affairs, Senator, Presidential Candidate, and Delegate to the Constitutional Convention of 1970. Since 1972 he has been a Visiting Professor at Cornell University and American University (Washington, D.C.) and a Fellow at the Center for International Affairs at Harvard University. He has recently returned to the Philippines.

His published works include *Freedom, Nationhood and Culture*; *Faith in the Filipino*; *Revolt Against Tradition*; *Land of Bondage, Land of the Free*; *Philippines: Silenced Democracy*; *Japan in Southeast Asia: Collision Course*; *A Pen for Democracy*; *Prospects for Philippine Transition*; and numerous articles in journals, newspapers, and magazines.